AT&T

SURVIVAL ROUTINES FOR FOR PROFESSIONALS

Moving Toward Corporate Success

THOMAS C. CANNON

AT&T Bell Laboratories

PRENTICE HALL, Englewood Cliffs, NJ 07632

Library Of Congress Cataloging In Publication Data
CANNON, THOMAS C.
    Survival routines for professionals.

    Bibliography: p.
Includes index.
1. Professional employees.   2. Career development.   3. Performance.   4. Interpersonal relations.   5. Success in business.   I. Title
HD8038.A1C36   1988   650.1   87-29067
ISBN 0-13-879271-2

Editoral/production supervision: Colleen Brosnan
Cover design: Ben Santora
Manufacturing buyer: Lorraine Fumoso

© 1988 by Prentice-Hall, Inc.
A division of Simon & Schuster
Englewood Cliffs, NJ 07632

Printed in the United States of America
10 9 8 7 6 5 4 3 2

ISBN 0-13-879271-2

PRENTICE-HALL INTERNATIONAL (UK) LIMITED, *London*
PRENTICE-HALL OF AUSTRALIA PTY. LIMITED, *Sydney*
PRENTICE-HALL HISPANOAMERICANA, S.A., *Mexico*
PRENTICE-HALL CANADA INC., *Toronto*
PRENTICE-HALL OF INDIA PRIVATE LIMITED, *New Delhi*
PRENTICE-HALL OF JAPAN, INC., *Tokyo*
SIMON & SCHUSTER ASIA PTE. LTD., *Singapore*
EDITORA PRENTICE-HALL DO BRASIL, LTDA., *Rio de Janeiro*

This book is dedicated to my wife, Joyce, who has given me four wonderful sons and who has nurtured the entire family through her aggressive management of family resources and her insistence on the well-rounded development of each family member. I sincerely appreciate her patience and support during the writing of this book.

CONTENTS

v

CHAPTER TWO

Typical Questions and Concerns of Young Professionals: Answers and Solutions 15

CHAPTER THREE

Organizing for Efficiency 53

CHAPTER FOUR

Skills to Acquire: Basic Tools of a Professional 63

C H A P T E R   F I V E

Things to Do: Suggestions on Personal Conduct and Interpersonal Interactions 87

CHAPTER SIX

Standards of Professional Performance 133

INTRODUCTION

This book is primarily written for individuals early in their professional careers in industry. It is also intended for professionals undergoing a job change or experiencing frustration on their current assignment. This book covers the things that must be learned, things that must be done, and skills that must be acquired in order to make the transition into a new job gracefully. (As such it represents an initial survival course.) It does not address long-term career development although it is clear that the two are related. The objective is to buy the new employee enough time to stay in the game until he or she learns the house rules.

A new employee, flush with the success of landing a new job, joins the organization with expectations for success. (Maybe a bit apprehensive, but still expecting to succeed.) After all, this person has faced tough challenges before and answered them with a series of successes, both in school and on previous jobs. With such a history, one takes on a new assignment with a gut feeling that hard work and smarts (and a break or two) are all it takes to make it   That attitude is wrong. One must first survive the cut.

According to recent statistics released by the U. S. Bureau of Labor Statistics, the nationwide turnover rate for employees of age 25 years and older is 22 percent per year. The corresponding rate for employees in the 20- to 24-year age bracket is 49 percent.

This high infant mortality rate, however, does not tell the entire story. Not all employees who do stay on have flourishing careers. This is due, in part, to differences in abilities among employees and to limited opportunities at higher levels in the company. Another contributing factor, however, is that some individuals get off to a good, but nonspectacular, start. Such employees often get categorized as "solid citizens." This is another way of saying that these individuals are valued employees, doing credible work, but are not likely to rise through the organization. Given enough time, such calibrations can be changed, but time is precious to all of us and it is to every employee's advantage to create strong positive impressions as early as possible in one's career. Thus the initial start affects the career trajectory that employees find themselves on. A good start can place employees on a steep upward slope whereas a poorer start can put them on a lower trajectory. A sketch of Pat Motola's model of career life cycles is given in Figure 1. Stated in the terms of this figure, the principal objective of this book is to increase the slope that a new employee rides on during the early stages of his or her career.

Making the transition into a new job is analogous to going from high school to college. After arriving on campus, a new student must get certain things established before it is possible to really move into high gear. One must first get settled in. By this I mean taking care of housekeeping issues such as registering, handling financial matters, arranging for transportation, and attending to other matters of an individual nature. One must also get plugged in. This includes identifying sources of support (academic as opposed to financial), becoming acquainted with key people (such as counselors, administrators, and student leaders), learning rules and regulations, and becoming familiar with the campus and community. Similarly, in any new assignment the employee must make adaptations and

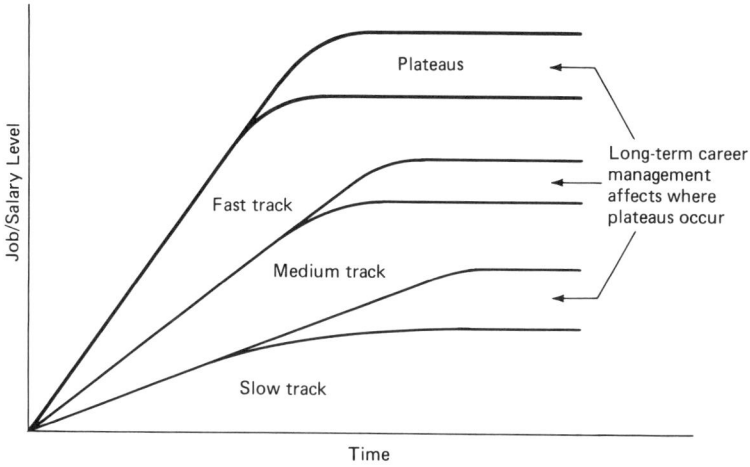

FIGURE 1 Corporate Career Life Cycle

take key actions during those critical first few months. But there is a difference between the two situations. Whereas many colleges have formal freshman orientation programs, such programs are rare in industry (and unevenly implemented). This book is intended to fill voids where they exist and complement company orientation programs that are already in place.

The new employee does not have the time or the luxury to learn survival principles late in the game. In the corporate environment, opinions are formed early and unsolicited feedback is given late. A formal performance appraisal (especially the first) may not come until a year or more after the employee performed the work. Such feedback may be too late for the new employee to modify his or her actions in a way that can affect calibrations. Compounding this problem and further underscoring the need for early education is that management forms perceptions on the basis of brief and infrequent contact. Calibrations formed during these contacts, supported by evaluations from immediate supervision, solidify judgments made on new employees. It is thus to the employee's benefit to be doing everything right during such meetings with management.

This text is organized into six chapters. Chapter 1, "Things to Learn," calls for a continuation of the thing that a professionals do best—learn. The emphasis in this chapter, however, is not on getting up-to-date technical knowledge in a particular area of work, but rather on learning things about the company and gaining perspectives that will allow the employee to work with better direction.

Chapter 2, "Typical Questions and Concerns of Young Professionals," examines the workplace from the employee's perspective and answers some of the most common questions posed by employees.

For neophytes in the business office, Chapter 3 provides basic tips on how to organize to work efficiently. Persons with previous work experience can skip this chapter without losing the continuity of the book.

Chapter 4, "Skills to Acquire," focuses on those individual attributes that may not have been required at all to do well in college, but are essential in the work place. These skills fall into two areas—how individuals relate to other people, and how individuals organize themselves to perform well on the job. In this chapter a strategic overview is given that deals with the objectives of various types of communications and how to better achieve these objectives. An important message delivered in this chapter is that the attributes discussed are, in fact, skills that can be acquired, as opposed to innate personality characteristics. They are essential skills that employees use (either effectively or noneffectively) throughout their career. And although some skills tend to improve with experience, they need to be in good working order immediately upon start of employment.

Chapter 5 deals with tactics and techniques for handling both the technical and interpersonal aspects of the job. The latter includes dealings with one's boss, one's peers, and with support personnel.

The final chapter provides guidelines to assist employees in getting a calibration on their performance level. The principal components of job performance are spelled out and performance scales for these components are presented. The chapter concludes with a summary of the most important things for a new employee to keep in mind. As such, the summarized items represent the key constituents of a formula for making a successful transition into a new job.

ACKNOWLEDGMENTS

I would like to thank Anthony Zamora of Purdue University for providing the initial stimulus to write this book. I deeply appreciate the detailed comments and suggestions made by Jim McCrory of AT&T and my Stanford University Sloan classmates Patrick Motola, Wataru Ogawa, and Janet Weatherbe, regarding style and content of the book. I am also grateful to Gene Webb and Jenifer Renzel of Stanford University for their thoughtful comments and encouragement. Finally, I will always be indebted to Elizabeth Rosen, Technical Staffing Specialist at AT&T Bell Laboratories, for her editorial comments, suggestions for improving the book's clarity and focus, and assistance in structuring the book to better serve the needs of its intended readers.

CHAPTER ONE

THINGS TO LEARN
The Company
and Its Business

Don't be misled. The first priority for new employees should not be to dazzle others with their brilliance, but to learn about the company and its business. Even though there's natural pressure on new employees to get up to speed quickly on technical activities in their work area, they must nevertheless put forth an intensive effort to learn company history, mission, organizational structure, work routines, performance evaluation routines, key contacts, values, and company jargon. Knowledge in these areas is essential if they are to have the perspective that will allow them to work effectively, efficiently, and with direction. This is such an important issue that some of the outstanding universities in the United States are devoting attention to it by including it in course material for students close to graduation. Richard Pascale, a professor at Stanford's Graduate School of Business, and Julian Phillips, of McKinsey & Company, Inc., have collaborated to develop a "Seven S Analysis" that future graduates must perform on their prospective employers. This analysis calls for an audit of the company's

Structure, Systems, Strategy, Skills, Staff, Style, and Shared Values and an assessment of how these seven S's will affect students' ability to be successful in their first assignment. This analysis, along with a 90-day action plan, induces the upcoming graduates to look at their new jobs in a structured way and thus diagnose (1) whether, in fact, a good match exists between them and the job, (2) the things that they need to learn and do before reporting to work, and (3) the critical issues that they must address during their first few months on the job.

Normally, immediate supervision takes the initiative in getting a new employee plugged into the technical aspects of his or her job. They may load down new employees with memos and reference material, introduce them to key people, and suggest ways of getting started. Too often it ends with that. If mentors or orientation programs do not exist, then the new employee must absorb nontechnical material on one's own. The responsibility thus often lies with new employees to continue and extend this process to ensure that they learn both technical and relevant nontechnical material.

It is a stressful period. At a time when the employee is adapting to a new work environment (and often undergoing a geographic relocation) he or she is being asked to absorb an overwhelming amount of information. But new employees have one thing going for them: They are being asked to do what they have shown they can do extremely well—learn. This chapter discusses the key things that must be learned.

COMPANY HISTORY: LET'S PUT THINGS IN PERSPECTIVE

Can you imagine some engineer going to work for Ford Motor Company without knowing that Henry Ford was its founder and that the Model T was its most famous early success? Or going to work for AT&T and not knowing of Alexander Graham Bell, or that the transistor was invented at Bell Laboratories? There are two points to be made here. The first is that all companies, large or small, take for granted that incoming employees have some knowledge of the company founders, product developments, and corporate affiliations. The second is that new people lacking such knowledge tend to be viewed as being less mature, lacking in depth, and having less commitment to the company.

A knowledge of the company's product line and history helps put current work in perspective. Knowing where you've been allows a better appreciation of where you are now, how you got there, and where you might be going. It gives the employee a better feel for what the business of the company really is. In addition to this, it allows the new employee to communicate better with one's peers.

Knowledge of corporate affiliations helps avoid conflicts of interest in business dealings, helps identify sources of support for projects, and helps assure that you won't say or do something that could embarrass other parts of the company.

COMPANY ROUTINES AND REGULATIONS: THE BEGINNING OF YOUR POWER BASE

Most large companies have documented routines and regulations governing administration, public relations, legal matters, ethical conduct, expenditures, employee issues (compensation, terms of employment, etc.), security, and sales. Often this information is compiled into one document and treated as the company bible. The principal thing that such a document does is to provide a road map of how to get things done within the system. It establishes boundaries of what can and cannot be done within regular channels. The company bible should be read. Scan through it when you first come on board just to get a feel for what is in it. You will then know whether to consult it or look for help elsewhere when some particular problem arises. Later on, when you are more familiar with company jargon and basic routines, it is a good idea to read thoroughly specific sections that affect your work.

In addition to the written law, there are informal routines that need to be learned that govern day-to-day activities. These include routines for obtaining staff assistance, generating written material, and obtaining management approval for action.

Procedures for obtaining assistance from staff organizations may be obtained by consulting with first-line supervision within each department or reading booklets that may exist describing the available services.

Written material must generally conform to an appropriate format and have some type of approval before release. Departmental secretaries have the best understanding of what these procedures are, and they are the most reliable source of information.

Procedures for obtaining approval for working on new projects, making purchases, taking courses, attending meetings, etc., may or may not be covered in the company bible. If not, immediate supervision should be consulted as the need arises.

WHERE TO FIND HELP

It is important to know what type of support systems the company has in place, who runs them, and where to find them. Although no two companies are structured the same, internal organizations tend to be classified as being one of two types depending on the nature of their activities. These two types are *line organizations* and *staff organizations.*

Line organizations are ones that have responsibilities directly associated with the products of the company. Their functions might include research, design, development, manufacturing, marketing, or sales. These organizations are held accountable for product success in the marketplace. Conversely, staff organizations provide the resources and support necessary for line organizations to do their jobs effectively. Typical functions include purchasing, payroll, accounting, security, records, legal, and public relations. In the words of Elizabeth Rosen, technical staffing specialist at AT&T, the distinction between the roles of the two organizations is that, "Line organizations move the world forward. This is the place where dynamic, leading-edge decisions are made. Staff organizations, on the other hand, make the world go round, providing stability. Staff is like guard rails on the expressway of decision making, establishing checks and balances to ensure continuity" (Rosen, 1985). Most programs that are designed to help the individual employee are administered by staff organizations. Some of the programs that are particularly beneficial to new employees are mentoring, counseling, affirmative action, and education.

Mentoring programs typically consist of a seasoned employee working with a new hire to show the person the nuts and bolts of getting things done within the company. It does not involve career planning. *Counseling* may be of the personal or career type. These programs typically provide coaching, mediation between employee and employer, assistance in career planning, and assistance in making transfers within the company.

Although *affirmative action* programs are designed primarily to help women and minorities integrate into the corporation, issues that affect members of other protected groups, such as handicapped individuals and Vietnam veterans, are also addressed. Affirmative action programs attempt to achieve better representation of people from protected groups in all levels of the company. To achieve this, special emphasis is placed on hiring, placing, developing, and promoting members of protected groups. All of this is done in an attempt to overcome imbalances that tend to self-perpetuate if left alone. Although targeted at members of disadvantaged groups, affirmative-action activities produce support mechanisms for all employees. Because those activities generally focus on nurturing people and finding better ways of dealing with issues affecting people, their solutions generally apply to (and ultimately benefit) all segments of the work force.

Education programs may have many facets. They range from formal plans that put the employee back in school pursuing a university degree, to short, company-administered, half-day seminars. In between there are courses that are tailored for the new employee, manager, or person seeking special technical or personal training. Such courses may be taught by university professors, company employees, or private vendors.

In addition to the functions described above, staff assistance can be obtained through library services, word processing, drafting, and personnel. Most company libraries are tied into a network through which they can quickly fill requests for books and articles, compile bibliographies, do translations, and perform a number of other special functions. Computerization allows drafting, word processing, and machine shop departments to provide functions to users that reduce errors, enhance work quality, and shorten the time to do jobs. Personnel organizations are geared to helping both existing employees and those being recruited. In addition to counseling and education already mentioned, personnel can provide information on employee benefits, relocation, and off-premises activities sponsored by the company.

The foregoing description of activities and division of responsibilities was presented to remind the new employee that he or she is not alone and help is available on a broad front. One way to get a feel for exactly what is available in your company is to scan the organizational section of your company phone book. Your boss and peers can help you interpret titles and organizational descriptions. Your local personnel office is the best single place to start collecting information on company programs and activities. If the personnel office doesn't have all the information, it can tell you where to get it.

ORGANIZATIONAL STRUCTURE: CHARTER, MISSION, AND CHAIN OF COMMAND

New employees need to understand the structure of their local organization and how they fit in with this structure. Specifically, they need to know occupational classifications, chain of command, and key interfacing organizations.

The author has known individuals who worked for months before realizing that their job classification was lower than that of other employees having similar educational backgrounds. Titles tell you very little. The best way to get a good understanding of the various classifications is to consult the personnel department, which should have an occupational listing, minimum qualifications for each level, and typical job descriptions. Information should also be available on salary ranges, authorization for expenditures, and support services that various levels are entitled to. (Don't be too concerned about presidential "perks" at this point in your career.)

Knowing the chain of command (both by name and face) and division of responsibilities can help in establishing job priorities. (It can also avoid an embarrassing show of ignorance.) It is not asking a lot to expect an employee to memorize six or seven names and titles. All employees should know their line of management up to the chief executive officer (CEO).

One quality that separates astute employees from ordinary ones is their grasp of "the big picture." What this really means is that they have taken the time to identify not only the role of their own organization but that of other interfacing organizations. The key questions to ask are: What organizations will be affected by my work? From which organizations will I require support in order for me to be successful in my job? What organizations are doing work that affects my activities? Is all this stuff being coordinated? If so, who is the central contact point for coordination?

Answering the above questions better assures that your work is headed in the right direction and will produce useful results.

JOB ASSIGNMENT AND HOW IT FITS IN WITH YOUR ORGANIZATION'S MISSION

Understanding how an assignment fits in with the overall mission of your organization gives insight as to what is really needed, what are the critical constraints, and what is the most desirable form of the solution. To help you fit the pieces of the puzzle together, ask yourself, "What will my contribution replace?" The answer to this question not only puts your work in perspective but also provides a standard against which your contribution can be measured.

Any time an employee is handed an assignment he or she should not walk away without answers to the following questions:

1. What is needed?
2. Who will use it?
3. What are the constraints?
4. Who will I be dependent on for support in this assignment?

5. What is the completion date?

Being told what is needed is not the same thing as being told in detail what to do. Managers are often guilty of overdefining assignments. That is, in their statement of the assignment they either establish so many constraints that a solution doesn't exist or they steer the solution down a particular path. Even worse, they may state the problem in terms of assumed constraints that may not be valid. Unfortunately, it is up to you, the inexperienced worker, to ferret out what is really needed (not just what is asked for) and to formulate the problem in terms that don't prejudice the solution. Before devoting too much work on the reformulated problem, however, it is best to get the boss's concurrence on the accuracy of your reformulation.

Know the customer. Presumably some *person* will use what you come up with, either an end customer of your company, or someone within your company who uses the results of your work in his or her job. A project is successful if the end product meets or exceeds the customer's expectations, is accepted by the user, and makes economic sense. By keeping in mind who the end user is, and how this person will make use of the product, you can better tailor the product to meet the individual's needs (or constraints).

Constraints fall into two categories—functional and developmental. Customers are a good source of functional constraints (such as size, price, performance, and features), whereas developmental constraints tend to be internally generated (such as budget, manufacturing cost, and compatibility). It is important that relevant constraints be identified and quantified when possible. Critical constraints (ones that drive the solution) should be challenged and validated.

Employees should understand what portions of their assignments fall within other people's responsibilities. Those dependencies must be identified before they can be managed. Knowing who they are allows employees to negotiate commitments for support and factor the time schedules of others into their overall schedule for the assignment.

The completion date is a critical, but often unstated, part of the contract. It therefore is important that time constraints be explicitly stated when you accept an important assignment. Inexperienced employees tend to be optimistic and place too much confidence in advertised completion dates of subtasks. Both worst-case scenarios and most-probable-case scenarios should be estimated. Scheduling errors, conflicts, and misunderstandings can be avoided if completion dates are spelled out in advance. Again, if such information is not volunteered, request it.

HOW WILL YOU BE EVALUATED
AND REWARDED?

In college the grading and reward system is well known and rather consistent throughout the country. Usually at the beginning of the course the professor describes the course work and states what it will take to get an A, B, or C. This is *grading*, or performance evaluation. The reward is getting credit for the course and having the grade appear on your transcript.

In industry things are not so clear-cut. First, managers practically never establish objective levels of job performance prior to completion of a project. Second, the reward is usually not guaranteed, is influenced by economic conditions, and may appear in a variety of forms (some of which may be unrecognizable to the employee). Thus it is common to find employees who not only don't know how they will be evaluated, but also don't understand the reward system. New employees owe it to themselves to understand how these processes work within their company.

Without a knowledge of the performance-evaluation process, employees may establish faulty job priorities, fail to impress the appropriate people, and misread signals they are given on job performance. Hence, they may not take advantage of opportunities to reinforce positive impressions or change negative ones.

There are several things that one needs to know about the evaluation process. First, who provides input to your rating? This may be rather complex. Even though only a small number of people pass judgment on your work, these judges may collect information from a variety of sources. Such information may come from members of management outside your organization who have had dealings with you, or it may come from customers or suppliers. Thus in one sense, everyone provides performance input. Acknowledging the reality of multiple sources of input, it still remains that only certain designated individuals have the responsibility to collect performance information, caucus, and come up with a collective judgment about your work. You deserve to know who these people are. Ask your management.

Knowing the cast of characters is a start, but you also need to know who plays the lead role. Who makes the final decision regarding the relative ranking of employees? Who is the person who sets the dollar value on your job performance? This information allows you to establish the range of management with whom you must stay in tune.

Another important element in the evaluation process is the frequency and timing of performance appraisals. Will you be evaluated every six months, yearly, or at some other interval? What is the time lag between job performance and job evaluation? This information will likely influence when and how often you request informal feedback on ways to improve your job performance. (It is not unreasonable for employees in their first year with the company to request informal monthly feedback sessions.) The timing of formal feedback may influence project planning and vacation scheduling.

The bottom line to all of this is how the performance evaluation affects your raise. (You may never find out because some companies consider the mechanics of making salary adjustments to be private.) Generally, job performance and employee classification interact with economic conditions, fiscal health of the company, and the job market to determine the amount of salary increases. A clear understanding of how this works helps the employee to avoid frustration and to establish rational objectives.

In summary, you need to know who provides input to your rating, who makes the final decision, when and how often you are rated, and how your rating affects your raise.

Raises are not the only means for rewarding good performance. There are, of course, promotions, special achievement awards, perks, increases in job latitude and job selection, and special assignments (such as being selected to receive special training, sit on special committees, or represent the company at trade conferences). The best way to find out what devices your company uses (and doesn't use) as rewards for outstanding service is to ask your immediate supervisor. You will then be able to better interpret the signals being sent.

KEY INDIVIDUAL CONTACTS

Often you must rely on individual contacts for getting information and obtaining support for your work. The most important individual contacts are either experts or people who act as interfaces. One type of interface is a person designated as project leader or coordinator. Such people generally have knowledge of what is happening on a broad front and can provide answers regarding product specifications, schedules, and responsibilities of others. You should spend the effort necessary to find out who the project leaders are in your area.

Managers, by the nature of their jobs, are interfaces. They are natural sources of information and support. It goes without saying that you should be acquainted with your own manager, but you should also know who the managers are in sister organizations (or organizations that share a business relationship). Knowing who these people are and what their ranges of responsibilities are will help you in getting the right input from the right sources when attacking an assignment.

Consulting recognized experts in your company is one of the best ways to get started on a project. It is part of doing your homework, and it demonstrates a degree of maturity. Aside from the cosmetic benefits, input from experts can improve work efficiency by (1) avoiding duplication of past work, (2) identifying reasonable ways to get started on assignments (so that you don't spin your wheels), and (3) providing direct assistance in solving specialized problems. You should therefore make an effort to find out who are the recognized experts in areas that relate to your work. Some large companies maintain a directory that lists employees who are considered experts or consultants in various areas. In other companies this network may be less formal but still exist. Supervision can often identify who the relevant expert is (or at least who is the most knowledgeable person) in a particular area. Thus "who's the expert?" is a natural question to ask at the time an assignment is handed out and when specialized assistance is needed during other phases of the project.

COMPANY LANGUAGE (JARGON)

Every company has its esoteric code words, jargon, acronyms, and phrases that are used in day-to-day communications within the company. Company jargon speeds up conversation and allows it to be more precise. However, people also use jargon to demonstrate their knowledge of the business and include themselves in a circle of up-to-date people who know what is going on. Conversely, if you become lost when the company code starts to fly, then evidently you must not be on top of things, and that is sufficient reason to exclude you from the conversation. (As you can see, the process is automatic.) Thus not only are you at a real disadvantage in keeping up with the conversation if you are unfamiliar with company slang, but such ignorance has some subtle implications regarding your perceived worth.

The best way to learn company jargon is to ask the user for an interpretation the first time you hear a new term. Make a note of it—mentally if not with pen and paper. (It won't be too long before you have a comprehensive LOA—List of Acronyms.) New employees can get away with asking dumb questions because they aren't expected to know the company language. However, the longer you wait to ask, the less gracious your co-workers will be.

If a glossary of terms is available, then it makes sense to review it, but usually such listings are either nonexistent, hard to find, or out-of-date. On the other hand, working documents either spell out acronyms explicitly or, by way of context, give the reader a clue as to what certain code designations represent. Even when interpretations are provided in documents that you have on file, it is a good idea to jot down these designations on your LOA. This will save you the effort of trying to remember at a later date just where and in which documents the interpretation is given. Further, just the process of writing them out will help fix code meanings in your memory. This compilation process should not go beyond about six months, and after nine months you should no longer need it.

CHAPTER TWO

TYPICAL QUESTIONS AND CONCERNS OF YOUNG PROFESSIONALS

Answers and Solutions

This chapter attempts to provide direct answers to some of the most common concerns of young professionals. Although the topics covered in some cases may only tangentially relate to success, they all have a great deal to do with the comfort level that an employee experiences on a new job. These topics relate to the lay of the land, how a new employee blends in with it, and general guidelines for early navigation.

HOW CAN I TELL IF THIS IS THE RIGHT PLACE FOR ME?

I'm glad you asked that question. It depends on a multitude of factors and their relative importance to you. You can answer this question for yourself by grading your company on two scales, one *absolute* and another *relative*. The absolute scale deals with the overall quality of the company, whereas the relative scale addresses how well your background, interest, and expectations match up with those of the company.

Company Quality

Let us deal with the company quality ranking first. As-sume that you've been on the job for a couple of days now and you have yet to be given a real assignment. In fact, you're start-ing to wonder if you are really needed. Chalk up a big negative "1" for your local management. They clearly aren't addressing a very fundamental issue on handling new employees and this may be an indicator of their overall lack of managerial quality.

MANAGEMENT'S ASTUTENESS

It is generally known that a new employee's initiation period is a critical time for making mutual reevaluations, shap-ing employee attitudes toward the company, and getting new employees oriented. Specifically, as Richard Pascale (1985) points out in his article on exploring the paradox of corporate culture, three important issues should be addressed during this period: (1) selecting and deselecting (screening and self screen-ing) of new members, (2) solidifying the commitment of new employees to the company, and (3) accelerating the socialization of new employees into the company culture. All of this is most efficiently accomplished by putting the new hire through an in-tense and demanding initial assignment. This tough phase helps management assess which new hires have what it takes to perform well with the company while at the same time it may cause some marginal individuals to decide for themselves that this may not be the right place for them. Solidification of com-mitment has been shown to be enhanced when new members of an organization are put through a tough initiation phase. Aron-son and Mills (1959) found in their study of college students that individuals valued their membership in a new organization more when they were subjected to a rigorous initiation period. Thus such treatment can promote employee loyalty and, all other things being equal, retention. Finally, by deeply sub-merging a new hire into some aspect of the company's work and giving that person intense attention during this period, the in-dividual learns more rapidly the shared values of the company and accepted ways of conducting business. It thus follows that a company that neglects this period is doing both itself and the new employee a disservice. Whether this neglect is due to ignorance, indifference, or special issues surrounding security clearance requirements, one's judgment of the company remains the same: a low score for the company in the area of people management.

HEALTH AND STABILITY OF THE COMPANY

Another factor that can be ranked on an absolute basis is the overall health of the company. Is the company among the leaders in its industry? Is the industry itself expanding or contracting? Is the company a likely takeover target? What has been the financial performance of the company over the past three fiscal periods? What is the trend? How does this performance compare to what has been happening to the overall economy and to what has happened to the industry? Answers to these questions will give you a feel for the company's stability and its prospects for growth.

AMBIENCE

Ambience is intangible but is nevertheless real. It is a subjective factor for ranking a company on the overall quality of the work atmosphere. It is a measure of how people feel about themselves, their work, and their fellow employees. It is manifested in how people interact with one another and the prevailing character of the work environment. If you find yourself saying, "There are a lot of nice things about working here" or "People seem happy here" or "I feel stimulated yet somehow relaxed," then give the place high marks on ambience.

OPPORTUNITY FOR ADVANCEMENT

A factor important to everyone is opportunity for advancement. This applies to opportunities through the professional ranks as well as into management. Here you must look at the structuring of the professional categories and the dynamics of your local organization. Is there room for professional growth outside of going into management? If you were so inclined, are there foreseeable management opportunities either inside or outside your local organization? Look around. What are the typical ages of persons in the senior professional categories and in first-level management positions? How old were they when they got promoted? Are these individuals entrenched in their positions (and possibly blocking advancement of others) or are they on upward trajectories? How do your capabilities compare to your peers? Answers to these questions will give you an indication of the time scale that is likely to be operating in your career progressions and the range of opportunities that you are likely to have. Companies that are more dynamic, that have shorter time scales, and have more flexible avenues for advancement should get higher marks.

How You and the Company Mesh

Match-up scales have to do with compatibility between you and the company. The two most important match-up items are geography and work preferences. Let us consider geography first. It is possible that, quite literally, some company may not be the right place for you. Geography is one element that you have to live with every day. Ask yourself how satisfied you are with the nature of the community, climate, cost of living, and array of activities available in the area. Would you want to spend the next five years there? How about the rest of your life? (It may never come to this but, nevertheless, is a reasonable question to ask.) How you feel about the external work environment can eventually overwhelm internal factors. Be reflective and search for how you really feel about where you must live and work. Ask yourself, "Would I be willing to live here if the job wasn't here?" (Be reasonable; everyone can't work in Hawaii.) If the answer is yes, then you are probably okay on the geography issue. Give the company a passing grade.

JOB MATCH

The other principal match-up item is very straightforward: Is this the job that you really want to do? Is it what you imagined it would be at the time of the interview? (Discount those unattractive tasks that go along with being in the training and orientation phase.) Are you working in an area that can make use of your best skills? If you can't answer yes to any of these questions, then you should consider making some sort of change. You basically have three options: a switch in assignments within the same organization, a transfer to another area within the company, and a change to another company. In considering changes inside the company you should step back, perhaps with the help of a company counselor or ombudsperson, and see if some fundamental problem exists that won't be eliminated by a transfer. Examine how well your skills and interest match up with the mainstream business of the company. This match-up affects both your potential advancement opportunities and the likelihood of your being able to work in areas that suit you over the long haul.

Corporate culture and personality compatibility are other match-up items worth considering. Corporate culture relates to collective values and accepted routines for conducting business. Take a look at how things are done around your company. Do the corporate values mesh with yours? Are the priorities ones you can support, and is the style one that you feel comfortable with (for example, highly structured routines versus the opposite extreme of free-wheeling operations, central control versus distributed authority, confrontational versus supportive)? Take a look at the personality types of people in leadership positions. Are they at all similar to you? Would you ever want to be like these individuals? If the answer to all of the above questions is no, then you'll likely be faced with some challenging readjustments.

Finally, take a look at the age demographics. Are there a significant number of other young professionals around? Will age differences cause you difficulty in relating to your peers?

When to Reach a Decision to Leave or Stay

Examining your new company in terms of the dimensions described above will allow you to assess for yourself whether or not you are with the right company. A good time to start doing this is during those first few days on the job. It is doubtful, however, that you will reach a point where you can come to a definite decision in just a few days.

When the Japanese talk about decision points they often mention what they call the four critical 3's; the third day, third week, third month, and third year. An example offered to me was that of newlyweds. On the first day of marriage, everything is wonderful. On the second day reality sets in (and sometimes disillusionment). Then on the third day, the newlyweds begin reflecting and reevaluating whether they want to continue with the relationship. The third day is a decision point. Furthermore, the decision made on the third day is revisited at the third week, third month, and third year. Getting past these points is critical for the survival of the marriage. In a very real sense the four 3's are turn-around points along the marital path.

The marriage analogy can be applied to many situations where an individual must make a significant commitment. Although the concept of the four critical 3's is obviously a generalization and oversimplification of what actually takes place, the concept is nevertheless useful in that it embodies (and, in fact, quantifies) two fundamental elements of the decision-making process: (1) reconsideration of prior decisions and (2) continued reconsideration at progressively longer intervals. The key implication is that if changes in course are not taken early, the issue may not be revisited until some distant point in the future after you have invested a considerable amount of time and resources. Further, after the third year, the probability of reversing your direction drops sharply. If you buy into this concept then you should carefully consider, as early as possible, whether your chosen career path is really worthwhile (that is, do you want to work in this company and in this activity?). Because it generally takes one year to learn most jobs, it may be asking too much for you to reach a decision in less time than that. However, the Oriental rule of four critical 3's suggests that you should come to some firm decision within three years. This nugget seems to contain a universal gem of wisdom.

HOW DO I GET PLUGGED INTO THE MAINSTREAM OF WHAT'S GOING ON WITHIN THE COMPANY?

Formal Programs That Help

There are many things that companies typically do for new employees that address this concern, and there are a number of things that you can do for yourself. Many companies have either formal or informal mentor programs for showing new employees the ropes. Sometimes the mentor is your direct supervisor, and in other cases it may be a more senior member of the staff. In any case, that person is charged with getting you acquainted with the technical aspects of your work and familiarizing you with company procedures. A good time to find out about such a program is during your initial meeting with the personnel department when you first report for work. A mentor program in itself will not assure you of being on top of things and provide you with a full awareness of what's going on in the business and what's lurking below the horizon. You can help yourself gain a better perspective by obtaining a business calendar of events. A business calendar of events? You say you weren't aware that there was such a thing? Of course there is; ask your boss about it. You say your boss hasn't heard of it either? She must have misunderstood you. She has one lying on her desk. It is contained in her personal calendar of appointments and upcoming events for the year. But you are only interested in those things that might affect you. Such events include performance evaluations, regularly scheduled work reviews or presentations, major trade conferences, special staff meetings, company-sponsored activities, and any events on your boss's calendar that may require your involvement or input. A good time to put together such a calendar is during your first meeting with your boss. When she invites you to ask questions or asks if she can assist you in any way in getting on board, you might reply that you would like to: (1) get a better perspective of the range of special activities that the organization is involved in and (2) become aware of upcoming events that affect members of the organization. A good start would be the major items on her calendar for the rest of this year and up until this time next year. She should be able to sketch out such a calendar for you at that time (bring a blank calendar along with you). If she wants to put more thought into it, she can get it to you later on in the week.

Informal Routes

So much for the formal routes. As we shall discuss in some detail in Chapter 5, much valuable information is exchanged over the lunch table. Get plugged into the lunch crowd if you really want to get in touch. Another informal network is employee organizations. These may or may not be company sponsored. Such activities are good opportunities not only to create friends but also to learn more about what is going on that you ought to be aware of. If you are a female or a member of a minority group, you might find that employee support organizations exist to promote communications among members and help enrich their work experience. Generally, membership in such organizations is open to all individuals regardless of sex, religion, or ethnic origin. You can find out about special clubs and company-affiliated organizations either through your supervisor or the personnel office. At that time you can also get a feel for how the company views such activities.

HOW DO I KNOW HOW WELL I'M DOING?

Employees typically have this question on their minds before they receive their first formal performance review. In well-run companies you shouldn't have to ask. Your supervisor should provide you with nearly continuous feedback during your progress on your first assignment. Ideally, your first assignment should be short, no longer, say, than three months, so that you can be given early indications of your apparent strengths and weaknesses, ways that you might improve, and how your current level of performance stacks up against what is expected.

Feedback needs to come early in order to correct poor performance and reinforce things that you are doing well. Informal feedback consisting of once-a-week reviews is not too often. In order to keep both parties relaxed, however, such meetings should not be cast as formal reviews. These meetings should serve the multiple purposes of keeping your boss informed, keeping the project on track, and, of course, providing your boss with the opportunity to give you corrective guidance and reinforcement. If your boss doesn't establish such meetings on his own, then you should request them. But be frank. Be explicit in letting him know the three benefits expected to be gained from such meetings.

WHAT CAN I DO IF I FEEL THAT MY WORK IS NOT BEING FAIRLY EVALUATED?

Voicing Your Disagreement

This question could apply to either informal reviews or formal evaluations written at any time during your career. The answers are the same in all cases. The scenario that I recommend is as follows: You should first identify just what are the points of disagreement, establish your basis for disagreement (discussed below), and then succinctly and dispassionately present your arguments to your boss. During this discussion you should take care to listen carefully to any rejoinder that the boss may offer. This willingness to listen can go a long way toward resolving differences.

If your disagreement cannot be resolved in this meeting then you are in trouble. You probably would be best advised to drop the issue at this point, but if you feel obliged to press the point you should proceed with caution and cool professionalism. What you need is a trusted and respected third party to serve as a mediator and hear both sides. In most situations this will be your boss's boss, but it could be a company counselor or ombudsperson. You should take the initiative to set up the meeting, first letting your boss know of your intentions and then contacting his or her boss to get on that person's calendar. You should prepare for the meeting by making notes that summarize points of disagreement and by giving some thought to what might be done in the future to avoid such disagreements.

When going into the meeting, be aware that it is against human nature for people to move very far from their initial position once that position has been formally taken. In psychological terms this is known as *anchoring.* Your boss is very human, and I've found that bosses typically have notoriously big anchors. The best thing that you can hope for is to get the person's attention so that you might get a more accurate evaluation next time. This being an objective, you certainly don't want to alienate your boss. Your conduct during the meeting should be as nonthreatening and as objective as possible.

Avoiding the Peer-Comparison Trap

One of the traps that you want to avoid is making assertions that you can't support; for example, judgments about the relative quality of your work compared to one of your peers. First of all, your boss will in all likelihood consider the discussion of other individuals to be a violation of their privacy and therefore inappropriate. Further, you don't have all the facts regarding the performance of others and what information you do have may be inaccurate. It is better to steer clear of such comparisons unless your boss brings them up.

Legitimate Bases for Disagreement

In any disagreement it is important to have a legitimate base of contention. This is especially troublesome in cases like performance reviews where many issues are judgment calls and thus difficult to contest. There are, however, some issues that are not based on judgment and can form the basis for your argument. Elements of the review that you can focus on are its completeness, accuracy, logic, and relevancy. Incomplete reviews typically lack balance. Balance means that strengths and positive contributions are mentioned as well as weaknesses and poor efforts. Not only does balance reinforce the good and identify the bad but it also fosters the appearance of objectivity, thereby increasing the likelihood that the person under review will buy into it. A review lacking balance can appear to be biased and therefore leave itself vulnerable to attack. Reviews can be incomplete in other ways as well. They can fail to mention activities that consumed significant portions of your time or special assignments. Sometimes such lapses are mere oversights. (A typical case is when contributions are made at the beginning or end of a rating period. Sometimes they are overlooked and sometimes they are counted twice.) If, however, these missing elements affect your overall evaluation, they should be corrected.

Accuracy, as the word implies, means getting the facts straight. For example, were you just a member of a team or did you, in fact, lead the work on the project? Did you innovate or implement (or did both) some new development? Did you undertake some activity on your own initiative or were you told to do so? (The implications can be either good or bad depending on the outcome of the work.) Was your work really part of a team effort or did you manage to get the job done despite lack of support from those charged with providing it? Was your assignment as simple as it was stated in the write-up or did it involve a broader range of activities, requiring multiple skills and thoughtful handling of nonroutine matters? Are the numbers and dates that are cited correct? (They need not be exact as long as the imprecision does not affect the conclusion that they are being used to support.) These are the type of questions that can be asked in examining the accuracy of a review.

Another item of the review that can be challenged is the logic. By their very nature, reviews tend to be on shaky ground in this area. The poor manager is put in a position where he or she must do a great deal of inductive reasoning. On the basis of only a sample of what a person can do, managers must infer what one's actual capabilities are. Small sample data give statisticians fits because of the relatively large variability that can be expected between different sets of observations. Nevertheless, undaunted by statistics, your manager must forge ahead, sometimes against your classic protest—"But that wasn't the real me!"—and form a judgment. (In the case of very new employees, managers can sometimes duck the issue for the first review and claim it is too early to tell.) After all, why should a manager logically conclude that you are a poor speaker just because you became catatonic when you stood up to give a presentation to the company vice-president? In all seriousness, sometimes it may be appropriate to challenge conclusions when either (1) the conclusion is based on a single event that does not reflect your true capabilities or (2) in reaching the conclusion, disproportionate weight was given to one particular occurrence (perhaps the most recent one) when other examples exist that support a different conclusion. In statistical jargon, "All the relevant data should be taken into account."

Other breakdowns in logic sometimes occur when addressing remedial activities. For example, a statement like, "Bill's writing should improve with practice; I'll encourage him to document more often in the future," sounds rather positive, but it exhibits questionable logic and ducks the question of what will be the mechanism for improving Bill's writing. It does not necessarily follow that Bill's writing will improve with practice. He may already be performing to the best of his ability given his level of training. Questions remain as to what the real source of the problem is and what the reviewer means by "encourage." It could be that Bill is so overworked that he doesn't have time to write or that he never really developed good writing skills (or both). A more logical and substantive statement might be, "Writing seems to be a burdensome task for Bill and he tends to avoid it. This, coupled with his heavy work load, has caused his documentation to lag. Both his skill and willingness to write may be improved by additional training in this area. I believe a course like the one offered in-house (or at a local university) would be helpful, and I therefore recommend that he enroll in the upcoming session. To allow time for this study, I am shifting out the start of some planned work. This additional time should also increase the likelihood of him wrapping up his existing projects with proper documentation." This is certainly a more lengthy statement, but it more logically addresses the perceived deficiency and doesn't shortchange the employee on the issue of career development.

Relevancy refers not to the validity of the criticism, but to whether the shortcoming is pertinent to your effectiveness on your current job or one that you might be expected to grow into. Your ability to perform arcane mathematical manipulations may be irrelevant to your effectiveness in conducting market research. Similarly, leadership skills may be relatively unimportant in someone hired to do state-of-the-art analysis in a highly technical area. The key issue is whether the perceived deficiency diminishes one's value to the company in the role (or roles) that one is reasonably likely to play. If it doesn't, then it should not be a part of the write-up.

Respecting Judgment Calls

The items discussed above are legitimate bases for disagreement on performance write-ups. You should keep in mind, however, that many issues dealt with in reviews are judgment calls and are difficult to contest. For example, most judgments on *level* of ability fall into this category. If you insist on pressing your disagreement with a review, be sure that you have a base of contention that others will view as legitimate.

Keeping the Right Perspective:
The Positive Aspects of Reviews

This section has focused on the possible negative aspects of performance reviews—addressing your greatest fears. A great deal more can be said about the positive aspects of reviews. Such items are covered in Chapter 5 in the section "Dealing with Your Boss." Over the years I have been involved in a great number of reviews, sitting on both sides of the table, and the overwhelming majority of these reviews have been uplifting experiences for both parties. I would say that my experiences are typical. The performance review is an opportunity for solidifying gains and planning growth. Though the benefits are intangible, the review itself is part of the reward system, namely, recognition and individual attention. The fairness and consideration that employees receive during such reviews affect how they feel toward the company and themselves and is manifested in the atmosphere of the workplace. Performance reviews are thus not the schizophrenic ugly face of the work environment, but rather a constituent of its visible image. You won't be surprised that often, and when you are it is likely to be positive.

WHAT AM I EXPECTED TO BE ABLE
TO DO?

The Four Components of a Job

Let us dissect the general content of a job to give you a better feel for what will be asked of you and illustrate how your training has prepared you for it. Most jobs can be divided into four components: (1) collecting information, (2) processing information (analysis), (3) making decisions and recommendations, and (4) implementing agreed-upon courses of action (including documentation and presentation). That's it. Where most young employees fall off the boat is that they fail to give proper attention to one or more of these components. This doesn't have to happen.

How Your Training Has Prepared You

Though it may not seem obvious, your college background has prepared you well to handle at least three of the four components, and the remaining one—making decisions and recommendations—is the one that you can get the most help with from your boss. Let us take a look at what college has done for you. First, it has taught discipline—the resolve to do what must be done and in the time frame demanded. Going through the rigors of learning on a tight schedule has taught you all about windows of opportunity and the importance of self-control. You are already a soldier. This discipline will help you in following through on the implementation component of a job.

Second, you have learned the terminology of the profession and can speak the language. This conversancy affects your ability to understand and be understood and thus helps you with the components of collecting and processing information. You already have this in your pocket.

Third, you are acquainted with the type of problems that people in your profession are confronted with and can recognize classes of solvable problems. You also have a bag of tools that can be methodically applied to solve such problems and have some idea where to look for help in solving nontraditional problems. Given the necessary information, you can solve the problem. Furthermore, you can recognize when essential information is missing. These skills are most helpful in handling the analysis component.

Finally, you are acquainted with library searches, how to access reference material, and generally how to go about collecting background information on a subject. These skills, together with ones previously mentioned, will help you with the information-collection component.

Things that change when you get to industry are that the territory is different and its dimensions are broader. For example, all of the relevant information is not neatly tucked away in the library. It may not even exist. One of the problems you must handle is identifying what the additional and relevant sources of information are. More, and different, dimensions are thus added to the information-collection component of the job. Factors such as health of the company, prior company commitments, legal restrictions, organizational constraints, and customer relations are just a few of the new variables that may enter into the decision-making component. You won't be expected to be immediately aware of all the new variables that may be operative but you will be expected to realize your ignorance. Your boss has a good knowledge of what extraordinary things must be taken into account. You only need to have the good judgment to ask the boss if there is anything missing in your formulation of the problem before you go charging ahead in search of a solution.

Summing things up, you are more capable than you realize. By considering all components of an assignment and giving proper attention to each one, you can better assure that you deliver on the things that others are counting on from you. Be sure to identify new sources of information and relevant variables. Don't go off the deep end without getting feedback, and don't hesitate to ask for help.

WHAT SHOULD I DO IF I CAN'T GET ALONG WITH MY BOSS?

Let's face it; bosses have different styles. They demand different things from their subordinates, vary in their priorities, and differ in their personalities. Even though people are selected for management, in part, on the basis of their ability to deal with a varied cross section of people, you nevertheless will perform better and be better appreciated if your style meshes with that of your boss. But what if they don't match? What do you do then?

Accommodation

Think about this for a minute. Over the course of your career you are likely to have many managers with differing styles. It won't be feasible to jump from one organization (or company) to another just because your style doesn't precisely mesh with your superiors. Therefore, by a overwhelming margin, your first choice is *accommodation*. (By the way, most of the recommendations offered here also apply to getting along with your co-workers.) Try doing things the boss's way. It won't compromise your integrity to do some things a different way and, who knows, you might learn something. It won't be forever. Company organizations tend to be dynamic in both their compositions and structure. Many crafty veteran employees realize this and employ the "wait-him-out" strategy in dealing with disagreeable bosses. They say to themselves, "Let's do it his (or her) way for now, make the best of it, and wait until he (or she) either self-destructs or moves on." This is a real-world survival routine. Sometimes in the waiting process the subordinates get converted and sometimes vice versa. The good thing about such a routine (that far outweighs the negative) is that it is accommodating. (The negative, of course, is the loss of effectiveness that accompanies lack of true commitment.) But it is better to be flexible. However, being flexible doesn't mean that you should never suggest to your boss alternate ways of doing things. It only means that you should not take it as an insufferable personal affront should your approach be rejected.

A mismatch in styles isn't all bad. Some potential exists for synergy to occur if you can complement your boss's strengths with strengths of your own. Think positively and look for such opportunities. Approach your boss by asking if he or she sees any benefit in your helping out in some particular area. Explain that you see this as a dual opportunity that would free him or her to handle matters that demand his or her direct attention, while at the same time be broadening for you.

Improving Your Motivation

Sometimes the problems that employees have with their bosses derive from employees' own lack of motivation. Employees may feel bored or stagnant in their jobs, and these feelings can in turn produce frustration and a loss of motivation. How do employees break out of this syndrome? One particular theory provides an answer.

David Nadler and Edward Lawler's (1977) Expectancy Theory of individual motivation describes how the reward for performance and the effort to achieve the performance level that leads to the reward combine to effect motivation. The theory is more complex than what is presented here, but the central concepts are as follows: (1) Individuals feel that the rewards they receive are contingent upon their achieving a specific performance level; (2) individuals assign a value or valence to an anticipated reward based on what the reward is worth to them; (3) an individual's motivation to perform is proportional to the product of three factors: namely, the valence of the reward, the probability that the individual can achieve the requisite performance level, and the probability that the reward will, in fact, be granted once the individual performs at the desired level. This last factor is not trivial. People are generally astute enough to realize that earning a reward is one thing, but getting it is another matter. Individuals therefore tend to subconsciously link the performance to the reward with a subjectively determined probability factor, say, $p(R/P)$, which stands for the *prob-ability* that the *Performance* will result in the *Reward*. For example, an employee may believe that if he or she achieves a performance rating of "outstanding," that there is a 50-50 chance of getting, say, a 12-percent raise. In this case $p(R/P)$ equals 0.5. In another example, a salesperson may feel that if she can convince her client's buying agent that her product is best for his firm, then there is a 95-percent chance that the purchase will be approved and she will make her commission. Here $p(R/P)$ equals 0.95.

The achievement of the required performance level also has a probability associated with it. The individual subconsciously assesses the probability that he or she can attain the level of performance necessary to have a shot at the reward. Call this probability $p(P/E)$, which is an abbreviation for *probability* that the *Effort* that one puts forth will result in the *Performance* needed to have a chance at the reward. Returning to our example of the salesperson, she might feel that given her sales ability, she stands a 70-percent chance of convincing the buying agent that her product is best for his firm. Here $p(P/E)$ equals 0.7.

A person's motivation to perform is the product of $p(P/E)$ times $p(R/P)$ times the cumulative valence (or value) that the reward holds for the individual. (Conceptually, the valence can be thought of as a number between 0 and 1 that rates the worth of a reward to an individual. A highly valued reward would have a valence of 1 whereas a lesser valued reward might have a value of, say, 0.7.) The cumulative valence is the total value of both the intrinsic rewards (that is, self-satisfaction) and extrinsic rewards (direct compensation) associated with the outcome. Completing the example of the salesperson, if we assume that the cumulative valence of making a commission of the sale is high, say, 0.9, then her motivational factor for pursuing the sale is approximately 0.6 (that is, 0.7 x 0.95 x 0.9 = 0.6). This model tells us that in order to improve motivation we must operate on one of the three factors in the multiplicative chain. Specifically, either the reward must be enhanced (by either changing its magnitude or switching it to something that has a higher cumulative valence to the employee), or the payoff probability, p(R/P), must be increased, or the probability that the effort will yield the desired performance level, p(P/E), must be increased. The employee herself can influence all three elements.

First she can renegotiate the reward with her boss. If the reward seems to be inconsistent with the amount of effort required, the employee might be able to switch the payoff to something of more value to her but is still within her boss's capacity to grant. For example, corporations generally have separate budgets allocated to different portions of its operations. In most cases managers have more latitude on how they can spend their funds for carrying on day-to-day operations than they do on granting raises. Thus in anticipation of only a moderate raise, the employee might negotiate perquisites (perks) such as a company-paid trip to a national trade convention or perhaps compensatory time off. (Such perks, of course, would be contingent upon attaining some agreed-upon performance level.) In other cases the reward may be a transfer to a more attractive job. In still other cases it might be possible to negotiate direct contingency increases in the raise itself. Whatever the case, increases in motivational level will be in proportion to increases in the valence of the outcome (as valued by the recipient).

The probability that you will, in fact, receive the reward after having attained the requisite performance level can be improved by establishing explicit agreements up front. Performance appraisals are the ideal times to make such agreements. At the end of the performance review, when you and your boss are making plans for your future growth, you should make known your short-term aspirations. At this time you need to find out what type of performance will be required to reach these aspirations. Both components, the performance level and the reward, need to be spelled out in as explicit terms as possible. However, be warned: Bosses are notorious for hedging on these types of agreements. They'll say things like, "Well, I can't promise you a promotion, but. . . ." This hedging is perfectly okay. You understand the uncertainty of the future and you don't want your boss to promise something that he or she can't deliver. But what your boss can promise you is that if you perform at a specified level for a specified period of time, you will be *rated* promotable. Usually this is as much as anyone can ask for. Another example of an explicit agreement would be a promise to get a part of a hot new project if you complete your existing project on time and within budget. The key is that explicit tie-ins made well up front will keep p(R/P) high, minimize misunderstandings, and reduce frustrations.

The final component that the employee can influence is p(P/E), the probability that the effort expended will result in the targeted performance level. This can be considered a productivity or efficiency factor. Productivity can be enhanced by either improving skill level or working harder. I prefer the former. Skill level can be improved through additional experience, training, and education. The route that you choose will depend on (1) the speed with which you wish to improve your ability and (2) job and family constraints. All other things being equal, additional education is the favored route because it also tends to give people fresh outlooks. Whether this education is paid for by the individual or the company depends on how the company views the economic payoff of the investment. (In some cases company sponsorship of additional education may be the negotiated payoff for attaining a higher performance level.)

Bringing things all together, employees can extricate themselves from boring or frustrating situations by improving their motivation. Motivation is influenced by the probability that effort expended will achieve the targeted performance level and that this performance level will in turn yield a worthwhile reward. Training and education affect productivity and the likelihood of achieving the requisite performance level. Up front, behavioral-specific agreements can help assure that the payoff will accompany the performance. Finally, expanding the definition of the reward (within the realm of what management can deliver) can make the reward have a greater valence for the employee.

Counseling

If accommodation just doesn't seem to be working and your motivation doesn't seem to be the problem, then the next step you should consider is counseling. Many large companies have employee career counseling organizations that can help you deal with the situation. Typically, they provide coaching and in some cases can help you obtain a transfer.

Give counseling a chance to work. Before giving up on ever resolving the conflict, make sure you can articulate to yourself just what the problems are and why they can't be resolved. Think about whether you have done every reasonable thing to improve the relationship. Think about how the situation might sound to a prospective new employer. Think about whether you would feel comfortable revealing to such an employer the true reason for your departure or whether you might be tempted to compromise your principles and cover it up with a lie.

I will return to my initial advice regarding accommodation. Try to maintain your perspective and flexibility. If your manager's methods are not illegal, immoral, or unethical, try to find ways to support them.

HOW CAN I BE SURE THAT MY WORK ADDRESSES THE RIGHT ISSUES AT THE RIGHT DEPTH?

This is an easy question to answer. Stay in touch with your boss. Draw up an outline of how you see the assignment and how you intend to tackle it. Be brief. Confine it to one page if at all possible. Be sure to indicate the depth of consideration that you plan to pursue on each major topic and what you visualize the end result will be. A review of prior company documentation on topics related to your assignment can give you a feel for what is generally expected. A projected completion date is a mandatory part of the outline.

Bounce this outline off your boss (or a seasoned peer, then your boss) and ask for comments. Now run with it.

HOW MUCH LATITUDE WILL I BE GIVEN
IN CARRYING OUT MY JOB?

For one thing, it depends on the company. But more than that it depends on the nature of your job, your immediate supervisor's style, general practices of your local organization, and the amount of confidence that management has in you. Do not confuse latitude with autonomy. Although you may be given considerable latitude in pursuing ways of attacking your assignment, you still might stay under constant supervision.

In most companies very few individuals enjoy the latitude to choose their specific assignments beyond working in a general area. Nevertheless, some companies do have policies that allow well-regarded contributors to have considerable say in what their specific assignments will be. (This is usually done in partial recognition for outstanding performance and demonstrated ability over a sustained period.) What it all boils down to is that the variation is so great between companies and even within the same company that the best way to get an accurate understanding of how much latitude you will have is to ask your prospective new supervisor during the job interview.

I'VE HEARD THAT MENTORS ARE IMPORTANT.
HOW DO I GO ABOUT FINDING ONE?

What Is a Mentor?

Mentors mean different things to different people. On one extreme a mentor can be thought of as someone who just helps you get on board by showing you the ropes while another view holds the mentor as someone who takes an active interest in your long-range career development. Most young professionals have their immediate supervisor as a built-in mentor. Some companies formalize this relationship for new employees by specifically designating the supervisor, or some other appropriate individual, as the mentor. These types of appointments address the short-term view of a mentor.

Long-Term Mentors

Long-range mentors are never formal arrangements. They occur when, through association and friendship, a senior employee takes a special interest in counseling, grooming, and promoting a less senior employee. The benefits that the lower-ranking employee derives from this relationship are matched by benefits to the higher-ranking individual which include having a chance to imprint his or her values and style on a potential young leader; keeping in touch with the thinking of new employees; gaining recognition for skillfully developing employees; and getting personal satisfaction from contributing to the growth of another individual. All parties win.

How Relationships Form

You say it all sounds great, but how do you find yourself a long-term mentor? To tell you that you should go forth and find thyself a mentor strikes me as a bit too Machiavellian. These relationships usually form naturally and the natural ways that they occur are not mysterious. They occur in the following ways: (1) *Common background.* People tend to associate with people like themselves. There is empirical evidence to support this happening in business relationships. Citing the findings of Domhoff (1967), Mills (1963), and Warner and Abbeglin (1955), Jeffrey Pfeffer (1983) makes the point that succession to leadership in major organizations is strongly correlated with social class origin. (What! Can this be true in a democratic society?) It may be deeper than this, but a simple explanation is that accession to leadership generally brings with it elevated social standing. Persons who attain such standing enjoy associating with others having similar backgrounds, and from this close relationships tend to form. (2) *Formal organizational relationship.* If someone recruited you then that person tends to have a vested interest in your success from two sides. First, this person wants to maintain a reputation of being able to pick winners; second, he or she would like to think that recruiting you was good for both you and the company. Other formal and sometimes unique business relationships can also lead to long-lasting mentorships. (3) *Common associate or interest.* Catalyst-like common interests are strong and persistent forces for bringing people together. Shared interest implies shared values, and knowing that another person shares your values is psychologically reassuring.

Summing up, the formation of mentor/protege relationships usually happens naturally and can benefit the company as well as the individuals involved. Though it is nice to have a long-term mentor, finding such a person should not be the uppermost concern of a new employee. Although you certainly don't want to duck opportunities to form such healthy business relationships, you shouldn't try to force them.

WILL I HAVE TO GO BACK TO SCHOOL TO GET AHEAD? IF SO, WHEN AND HOW?

Considerations

A fundamental reason for getting additional education is to expand (or renew) your capabilities so that you can be more effective in handling your current and future assignments. But there are other reasons as well. Additional education can provide the credentials that qualify you for consideration for a broader range of jobs, including promotion. It can also help differentiate you from your competitors and in some cases can help stimulate a stagnant career. (Of course, there is always the case where additional education is a formal job requirement that presumably relates to work effectiveness. In this case the rules are usually spelled out in rather specific terms and few options are left to the employee. This discussion will focus on only those cases where education is voluntary.)

In deciding whether to pursue additional education, there are several questions that you should ask yourself. One is: What other options are available for achieving what I want? Education is often viewed as a shortcut to promotion, but in many cases it may not be. What matters to your employer is your actual job performance. Additional education is an indicator of greater potential but in itself does not ensure improved performance. You might actually lose status with your employer if in the process of getting added education the quality of your work diminishes. Demonstrated capability on an actual

work assignment is the most convincing argument for advancement. Accordingly, if advancement is your objective, you might
consider whether a well thought out plan for work assignments
might better serve the role of developing (and demonstrating)
your capabilities. Your immediate supervisor can help you in
making this type of judgment and giving you input to such a
plan.

Other considerations are the "windows of opportunity" on
the job. Companies and businesses go through cycles of high
and low activity. In some cases new developments may be
emerging that can benefit individuals contributing in that area
at that particular time. In such cases it may be strategically
wise to stay as close to the action as possible. Dividing your attention between school work and your regular job duties could
be enough of a distraction to cause you to miss a perfect opportunity. You thus want to consider what momentum, or potential opportunities, might be lost by pursuing additional education at this time.

Another consideration is how the added load of school
work might affect your personal life and the lives of those
around you. Costs are not always measurable in economic
terms. Time spent on studies necessarily comes at the expense
of time that could have been spent elsewhere, including that
needed to maintain close personal relationships. You should
weigh this factor in reaching your decision.

Which Route Is Best: Part-Time
or Full-Time?

Should you decide that the timing is right and it is in your
overall best interest to return to the classroom, then you must
further decide which route to take—part-time, full-time, day or
night, degree or nondegree option? Night classes fit more easily
into your work schedule but crowd your personal time. Because students attending night classes tend to have more dis-
parate backgrounds than day students, the academic objectives
of night courses tend to be more modest than equivalent day
courses. If you are able to get time off from work during the
day, then this may be a more attractive route. Although the

work load may be heavier and the competition stiffer, you'll have more time to put into it.

IMPACT ON YOUR JOB

One thing that you have to watch out for is how will taking such time off during the day affect your treatment on the job. Despite the good intentions of your employer, in all likelihood you will get fewer high-priority assignments, and some managers might have difficulty assessing the weight of your contributions (based on, say, an 80-percent work effort) relative to the full-time effort of your peers. No general rule can tell you which route is best in all situations. However, in arriving at a decision you should weigh the above considerations carefully.

The decision that requires the most reflection is whether to go back to school full-time. A number of factors need to be considered. First, where are you on the raise curve? Professional salaries tend to flatten out as a function of years in grade. New hires typically get sharp salary increases their first few years on the job. The magnitude of these increases (percentage) starts to decrease after four to seven years in the same job classification and becomes virtually flat after 10 to 15 years. The average raise after this point usually is just equal to or below the inflation level. Obviously it is to your advantage to stay on the steep portion of the raise curve for as long as possible. The only way to do this is to get regular upgrades in your job classification. Such changes are thus the eternal fountain of youth for professionals. A promotion can transform an old accountant into a new partner and a senior engineer into a young manager. If available, look at your company's pay scales and growth trajectories for different job levels. If another college degree can help you advance into a new classification, it may be worth pursuing because of the high growth factor, even if the promotional pay increase is not large. Sometimes an added degree will actually limit your options. Becoming more specialized may qualify you for a higher-level job in a particular area, but it may also make you less attractive for jobs outside that particular area. Your added education may be viewed as a step toward specialization. In general, specialists are not thought of as future managers except in highly technical areas.

HOW DO I HANDLE SEXUAL HARASSMENT?

Let us begin by examining what constitutes sexual harassment. The Equal Employment Opportunity Commission issued guidelines in 1980 defining sexual harassment as

> Unwelcome sexual advances, requests for sexual favors, and other verbal or physical conduct of a sexual nature. . . when (1) submission to such conduct is made either explicitly or implicitly a term or condition of an individual's employment, (2) submission to or rejection of such conduct by an individual is used as the basis for employment decisions affecting such individual, or (3) such conduct has the purpose or effect of unreasonably interfering with an individual's work performance or creating an intimidating, hostile, or offensive working environment.

Item number 3 is the definition that is most encompassing and also the most subjective. Because of this subjectivity, more needs to be said to clarify more fully what constitutes harassment.

Sexual harassment is action taken against another individual because of that person's sex. It is either coercive, solicitous, disparaging, or has the effect of creating emotional or physical trauma. The key factor is *the effect* that such actions have on the recipient, not the intent of the initiator. (It is not all right for people to say or do whatever they wish as long as their intentions are good. They must also consider what effect their actions might have on the other person.) This is where confusion often arises. Different people have different sensitivities and differ in how they might interpret actions of others. This being the case, it is incumbent upon someone who might be viewed as an aggressor to ensure that one's behavior does not convey signals that may be construed as sexually harassing. You might ask, "What's safe and what's taboo?" The answer is that there are certain gray areas where individuals are advised to tread carefully, and other areas that are strictly off-limits. The gray areas include touching, making remarks about another person's physical appearance, probing for receptiveness to personal involvement outside of normal business interactions (a pass), making inquiries about someone's personal relations with other individuals, flirting (through verbal and nonverbal means), infringing on someone's personal space (getting too close), and making requests or invitations that are void of explicit sexual content but, nevertheless, are of a personal nature and unusual in the business setting.

Areas that unmistakably fall in the harassment arena include lascivious comments about another's physical appearance, persistent advances, physical contact of a sexual nature (pats, pinches, and unusual caresses), direct sexual propositions, wolf whistles, the display of sexually suggestive material, and pejorative comments of a sexual nature directed toward another individual. (A word of clarification: The use of vulgar or abusive language may be interpreted as sexual harassment even though it may not be directed toward any specific individual or group of individuals. Such behavior generally violates canons of professional business conduct and may infringe on the rights of some individuals as defined by equal employment opportunity and affirmative action regulations. This is especially true if such language is used as a means of badgering certain employees to make the work environment less comfortable for them.)

Sexual harassment in the workplace is destructive in several ways: It is psychologically damaging to its victims, it poisons the work atmosphere, and it lessens productivity by forcing its victims to wrestle with issues other than business matters. There is also lost efficiency caused by managers having to devote time and effort policing and resolving these conflicts. Well-run companies recognize the destructiveness of sexual harassment and generally have prescribed routines for handling such cases. Nevertheless, transgressions do occur. You, the victim, may find yourself in a position where you must: (1) make a real-time response and (2) take some action to prevent further aggression. How you should handle this depends on the nature of the affront and its source. Throughout this section I will assume that the harassed person is a female. Although this may not always be the case, historically it has been the one most commonly encountered. Accordingly, in order to be of greatest benefit to the reader, this discussion will focus on the most prevalent case.

To understand what responses will work best, let us examine several factors that might contribute to sexual aggression. We are not concerned with identifying the source of the sex drive, but rather understanding why sexual aggression might surface in the workplace. The high level of self-confidence that goes along with either being in charge or being on your home turf may account for some harassment. Research done by Reis, Wheeler, Spiegel, Kernis, Nezlek, and Perri (1982) showed that physically attractive men initiated more contact with women, but the amount of contact was mediated by their degree of self-confidence. Thus it is possible for an individual to be sexually aggressive in one arena and not as aggressive in some other setting where he doesn't enjoy the same amount of self-confidence.

Another possible explanation for sexual aggression that shouldn't be overlooked is simply ignorance. Barbara Gutek (1985) found in her study on sexual harassment that most men believed that women felt ". . . complimented and flattered by advances from a man, especially an attractive man." To the contrary, 63 percent of the women questioned reported that they were insulted by such advances. Gutek refers to this as "the giant gender gap." This disparity immediately suggests that a possible starting point in defending against sexual harassment is to make sure that the offender clearly knows that such harassment is insulting and offensive.

Still another factor is availability. For some men the workplace may offer more abundant interaction with females than any other milieu in which they circulate. Furthermore, they don't have to go out of their way to initiate such contact.

Perhaps the most disturbing factor that might contribute to sexual aggression is the need for dominance and control. Basically this is a need to feed the ego through a demonstration of power over another individual. In this sense it is much akin to rape. In such a scenario, rejection nearly equates to a challenge of power and therefore must be handled in a special way if negative consequences to the victim are to be minimized.

The tactics that you employ in response to sexual harassment will depend on its source. For most problems that you encounter at work, your boss will be your first source of help. In some cases, however, the person doing the harassment may be your boss. You thus need to be prepared to handle aggression from individuals within and outside of your chain of command.

Aggression from a Peer

Your response must be consistent with the threat. As already indicated, acts such as touching, making suggestive remarks, and even staring can be interpreted as sexual harassment. However, the context of such acts and how you feel about the other individual may influence your perception of its severity. Accordingly, I won't attempt to make absolute judgments to classify the seriousness of each form of harassment. You will have to make such judgments yourself and adjust your response to be consistent with the perceived magnitude and nature of the threat. In these cases it is important that your response be measured. Overreacting can give you an unwanted reputation as someone looking for trouble, whereas underreacting can encourage further advances.

MILD, PERHAPS UNINTENTIONAL,
HARASSMENT

Responding to everything that might possibly be viewed as harassment can cost you not only your credibility but also may make others reluctant to work with you. You will have to make the call as to whether sexual harassment was actually intended. When in doubt it is best to respond with a brief, chilling stare or a statement like, "I don't know what you meant by that and I won't press you for an explanation. Let's just leave things at that." You can't afford to just ignore the incident. (A 1975 survey conducted by the Women's Section of the Human Affairs Program at Cornell University revealed that 75 percent of the time that harassment was ignored it eventually worsened.) No response might cause the person doing the harassment to think that either you didn't hear him, missed his subtle pass, or, in fact, are receptive to further advances. Get the message across that you do not find any humor in the situation and you are not interested in him, but do so without making a direct accusation.

DEFINITE, UNMISTAKABLE HARASSMENT

In order to protect yourself, you must take definite and official action. Let the other party know at the time of the incident that you feel that the person is out of line, that you don't like it, and that you will take whatever measures necessary to ensure that you are not harassed by him in the future. (Use the word *harassed* to ensure that he understands your framing of the incident.) Document the incident by writing down your description of what happened and arrange a meeting with your boss. Ask the boss's advice as to what you should do. Make a note of this conversation, being sure to include agreed upon action items, if any. (Sounds like a lot of work. Maybe, but this is serious business.) Give things time to straighten themselves out. Document any repeat episodes and follow the routine described above. If the situation doesn't improve you should press your boss for higher-level involvement or assistance from an appropriate staff organization in the company. This is where the documentation is essential. It establishes the habitual nature of the harassment and the fact that the company had been made aware of what was going on.

You must be prepared to play out the hand. The big concern of female employees in situations like this is that the conflict will be resolved by transferring her out of the organization or putting pressure on her to resign. (History has shown that such fears are well founded.) Neither of these outcomes may be acceptable or fair to you. A recourse is to initiate legal action to either preserve your position, compensate you for damages, or both. Legal action, however, should be viewed as a last resort and should never be used just as a threat. Title VII of the 1964 Civil Rights Act prescribes some protection for women against sexual harassment. You should consider legal action if you find that you are not getting support from your company and you don't feel that others are acting in good faith.

Sexual Harassment from Your Boss

Clearly the most threatening source of sexual harassment is from your boss. Unfortunately, it is also rather common. Barbara Gutek found in her study that in 45 percent of the cases of sexual harassment, the initiator was the immediate supervisor. Your boss is the person whom you must look to for guidance and depend on for protecting your professional interest. As such, he occupies a very powerful position in your life. Sexual exploitation of a subordinate by a superior represents the ultimate abuse of power. The question to be answered is,

"How do I maintain my integrity yet not be disadvantaged because of residual ill feelings between me and my boss?" The answer lies in being able to walk a very narrow tightrope. Fortunately, females have facilities and characteristic response patterns that can be of tremendous help in fending off this type of aggression. These strengths, however, must be recognized and marshaled in a constructive fashion if you are to maximize their benefits.

An advantage that women tend to have over men in emotionally charged situations is the ability (and willingness) to articulate their feelings. This should not be suppressed. Because of the ignorance factor that exists in Gutek's gender gap, it is important that you make the other party clearly understand just how you are being affected by what the person is saying or doing. The more clearly this message is conveyed, the better the chances are that the other party will take time to reconsider what is happening and put the interaction in a more rational perspective. Another advantage that women have is their tendency to think in terms of long-term relationships. More specifically, they intuitively consider how resolution of today's conflict will affect future relations with others. In cases of sexual harassment this is a crucial, if not the most important, issue. How are things going to be further down the road? What can I do now to shape the relationship into one that is acceptable to both of us in the future? Because they are more inclined to take the long-term view of interpersonal relationships, women tend to be better tuned into the critical issue that ultimately has to be addressed.

YOUR "REAL-TIME" RESPONSE

It is important that your first reaction convey the proper message. What you actually say will be conditioned by an entire array of variables such as prior relations between you and your boss, the nature of the overture, its setting and context, your boss's personality, and even your marital status. But what you want to convey is cool professionalism. Get your feelings understood, but with as much emotional detachment as possible.

Messages you want to deliver. Specific points you may want to get across are:

1. You don't share his feelings.
2. It is upsetting to you that he is thinking of you in sexual terms as opposed to strictly professional ones.
3. You are not at all flattered by his sexual interest in you and, in fact, are quite disturbed by it.
4. You had hoped that in this company you would be able to contribute without regard to sex. You view his actions to be in conflict with company standards of behavior and even with his own personal image.
5. You think that both of you need to sit down with company counselors to work through this conflict. (This is a mild threat.)

You may also want to be sensitive to his feelings and provide him with a way to retreat gracefully. For example, you might say, "I know you well enough to be certain that you would never think of pressuring one of your subordinates for sexual attention. I therefore am discounting the possibility that any pressure was intended, but rather, your actions resulted from misinterpreting the basis for our friendship. My feelings toward you remain, as always, as those of one professional toward another. I value your friendship, but in a nonsexual way."

You should make it clear that a degree of trust has been lost between the two of you. It takes a long time to build up the trust that he, not you, has damaged, and it is his responsibility, not yours, to rebuild that trust again. Let him know that traumatic episodes like these take a long time to forget (in reality, they probably are never forgotten) and that it is going to be harder for you to put this incident behind you than it will be for him to part with any long-term grudges. For the relationship to survive, you will both have to work hard, but on different issues.

Pitfalls you want to avoid. In carrying out your real-time response, there are certain things that you want to avoid. First, don't lecture him. No matter how agitated you may feel or how emphatically you say it, he is not going to be "ashamed of himself"; he is not going to sprout renewed religion, rise to a higher level of professional ethics, or feel more devoted to his wife. And he is not going to be receptive to arguments about how unattractive you are and why he shouldn't be interested in you in the first place. Lecturing him can only drive a deeper wedge between the two of you, generate more emotional discussion on the topic, and make it more difficult for this entire episode to be dealt with and forgotten.

Second, don't overtly threaten him. Although a threat may actually be effective in getting you immediate relief from harassment, it may be at the expense of making future relations even more strained. You don't want to form a powerful, long-term enemy if you can help it (which you may not be able to avoid, no matter what you do).

Another thing you don't want to do is make apologies for his aggression. For example, don't say, "I'm sorry if I did anything that led you to believe that I had a romantic interest in you." Statements like this one can be twisted and used against you later on. The aggressor might say that even you admitted that the whole thing might have been your fault. Don't give him any ammunition.

Finally, don't fall into the trap of trying to provide excuses why you can't comply with his demands. By offering excuses you are tacitly legitimizing the advance. Further, excuses have the effect of shifting the focus from your right not to be harassed to the false issue of resolving some problem that stands in the way of him getting what he wants. This not only opens the door for more debate but also leaves you vulnerable to counterarguments. For example, he might counter your excuse that he is married with any number of explanations regarding the relationship between him and his wife (they have an understanding; she doesn't understand him; she doesn't love him; he doesn't love her; they are in the process of breaking up, and on and on). He might counter your argument that it is against your policy to date business associates by pointing out that others do it or by attacking the rationality of such a policy. Such an argument could also make things tense for you in the future should you find a business associate that you would earnestly like to date. All excuses suffer the same fundamental weakness—they shift the conflict from an infringement on your individual rights to a more antiseptic issue of changing your personal policies. There is only one excuse that may be worth using—you are married. (Even this excuse, however, has some risks. Your protection could suddenly evaporate should your marital status change.) The principal benefit of the marriage shield comes not from the unassailability of your convictions, religious or otherwise, but from the threat of uncertainty that accompanies a third person entering the picture. While the aggressor might feel confident that he could handle any situation that might develop involving you, the company, and himself, he may feel less in control in interactions involving your spouse. You can fuel such discomfort by pointing out that you don't keep secrets from your husband and you don't know how he is going to react when he learns of this.

Before you end this discussion, you should try to get a reading on what future relations are likely to be between the two of you. Be frank. Tell him that you don't know how this episode will affect your future working relations and you would like to know how he feels about it. Listen to what he has to say and, having already given it your best shot, leave things as that.

ACTIONS TO TAKE AFTER THE
CONFRONTATION

So much for real-time responses. Regardless of what went on in your discussion, you have some homework to do. As in all cases like this, the first thing you must do is document to your best recollection what was said and done. (Do this as soon as you can to guard against details fading from memory.) It is not that you are trying to hang anybody; it is just that you don't know how things are going to turn out. A written account of what took place can help you in two ways: (1) It can provide a basis for discussing your problem with others and (2) it can help you substantiate your case should things get ugly. A hand-written, dated account is sufficient.

The next thing you want to do is find out what help is available within the company. Likely sources for such help are your company's equal employment opportunity counselor, affirmative action organization, and the employee career counseling group, if one exists. If help is available, use it, no matter what you had to agree to regarding silence in order to get out of your boss's clutches. Even if your boss apologized and said all was forgotten, you have no assurance that things have been completely put to rest. You have no choice but to use whatever assistance is available.

Practices vary among companies. When you approach such organizations, be guarded with your information until you know how the information will be handled; who will have access to it (confidentiality), and what wheels will be automatically set in motion by your revealing it. More specifically, you need to know what are the prescribed company routines for handling such cases, what has been the outcome of recent cases of this type, and what will be demanded of you. Such proceedings are never without risk. You need to know from the start what the risks are.

One thing you want to keep in mind is that your principal objectives are to protect yourself (physically, emotionally, and professionally) and to resolve the conflict at the lowest possible level. It is not to extract a pound of flesh. Keeping a positive and professional frame of mind will help you emerge from this experience with both your own self-respect and the respect you command from others intact.

You must also have in mind what you believe to be an acceptable final outcome. Should your boss be removed? Should he be reprimanded? Should he be transferred? Should you be transferred? If your boss stays and ill feelings remain, then you should press for a transfer. As mentioned earlier, employee counseling organizations within the company can sometimes provide assistance in doing this. If you feel that a transfer would place an unfair burden on you or would be otherwise unacceptable, then you may have no alternative but to consider finding a job elsewhere. As in all cases of this type, before the situation stimulates you to leave the company, seek outside legal advice to help you assess your rights.

CHAPTER THREE

ORGANIZING
FOR EFFICIENCY

A number of housekeeping procedures can improve your efficiency in day-to-day operations. For the most part they are merely habits you can adopt that become integral parts of your personal business routine. These habits take a little more effort to establish initially but, as with all habits, in time they become automatic and almost effortless. The payoff is both improved efficiency and decreased likelihood of things falling through the crack.

DAILY LIST OF THINGS TO DO

Making a daily list of things to do is easy. The best time to do it is in the morning when you are fresh and energetic. It doesn't matter which items you list first just as long as the list is complete. It doesn't have to be elaborate; cryptic notes that are understandable to you are all that is needed to remind you of unfinished tasks.

Which items you tackle first is up to you. You may prefer to work on the most urgent matters first or the most important ones. To reduce the number of items hanging over your head, you may want to start by clearing the deck of small items first. On other days you may prefer to work on items that suit your mood that day. (This is one of the luxuries of being ahead of schedule on your projects.) Research done on how mental efficiency varies during the day has shown that your powers of analytical thinking are greatest in the morning. Accordingly, you might want to use this time to perform tasks involving mathematical analysis, heavy reading, or writing. It really doesn't matter how you tackle the list as long as you meet your commitments on time. (It is not a good practice to wait habitually until the eleventh hour to start every assignment.)

There are only three periods during the day when you can count on not being interrupted: in the morning (up to 15 minutes after the start of work), during the lunch period, and after work. You may want to plan to do some of your tasks during these time sanctuaries.

Finished items should be completely scratched off the list. Just checking them off is not good enough. They are still there and clutter up the list when you look for the next item to work on. Totally scratching through them emphasizes their completion and allows you to focus more quickly (and intensely) on remaining items.

Items not completed one day should be carried over to the next. Don't feel compelled to start a brand new list every day. Besides, the old list may contain a lot of useful data like phone numbers, dates, and other notes that you don't want to bother recopying every day. You can continue to use the same list, with daily updates, until it has outlived its usefulness.

ROUTINES FOR USING THE PHONE

There will be some people who you will know only as familiar voices on the other end of the phone line. Likewise, they may only know you by your voice, manners, and how you carry out a business conversation. To these people, how you come across over the phone is how you are. Accordingly, you want to appear just as professional over the phone as you do in person.

The phone is a great time saver, but it is a double-edged sword. It can just as well waste your time. It helps to know techniques for maximizing its utility and minimizing its detractions. Since some readers may skip this chapter, some of the advice presented here on making and receiving phone calls is repeated in Chapter 5 in the section titled "Cultivating a Positive, Alert Image."

Making Phone Calls

Some people are hard to catch in their office. The best time to reach anyone is at 8:50 A.M. (or 20 minutes after their scheduled start time). This is late enough to allow them to get settled in at their desk but early enough to catch them before they get involved in meetings. (It's also a time when people like to be at their desk to show their boss that they made it into work on time.) Because most early morning meetings start at 9:00, a call at 10 minutes before that time allows you to conduct a brief conversation before the person you phoned has to leave.

It is proper business etiquette to always identify yourself and company affiliation before asking to speak to the other party. For example, you might open with, "Hello, this is Dave Miller of American Hardware Supply. May I speak to Richard Davis?" The person (or machine) answering the phone could be anyone. It could be his secretary, a receptionist, his office mate, or Dave himself. If you can't reach the person directly and the individual handling the call doesn't volunteer to take a message, go ahead and ask if you may leave one anyway. Aside from your name and phone number, make sure you say what the phone call is about. If all you want is an answer to a simple question, then state the question so that the person you phoned will be prepared with an answer when he or she returns your call. Even if you are away from your desk when the party returns your call, he or she may be able to get the answer to you by leaving it with the person who answers your phone. In cases where you absolutely must speak directly to the person you're calling, try to avoid playing "telephone tag" by finding out when it is a good time to catch the person and by leaving word as to when you will be at your desk.

Receiving Phone Calls

You should be geared to take notes when you answer the phone. When the calling party tells you his or her name and company, jot this information down as quickly as possible. Make sure you get the first name down correctly for you will be using it during the conversation—especially at the end. (You needn't interrupt if you don't quite get everything at first. You can fill in the missing information sometime before the conversation ends. For now, scribble down something reasonably accurate and continue listening.) Also make sure that you have a clear understanding of what the other party wants. Taking notes as the other person talks will help you focus on doing this and ensure that you retain important information. You can explain delays in your responses by letting the caller know that you are taking notes (which the caller will assume anyway). Get the other party's phone number and the correct spelling of the name before you hang up. It always makes people feel good when you use their first name in closing. (You won't have to fumble for it if you've written it down initially.) A natural closing like, "Very good, Bill. I'll be getting back in touch with you. Goodbye," provides a crisp, yet personal, ending to a conversation.

Courtesy to an Office Mate

If you share an office with another person, there will be occasions when you may have to answer that person's phone when he or she is out of the office. When you do this you want to remember that you need not volunteer that person's whereabouts unless the calling party legitimately needs to have this information. For example, when the calling party asks to speak to Ralph, you need not reply with, "Ralph's not in yet," or "Ralph's still out to lunch," or "Ralph's gone home already." It is sufficient to reply, "Ralph is away from his desk right now. Can I take a message?"

On the other hand, if it is an important message and you know your office mate's whereabouts, you should take the time to locate the person.

The point here is that you want to forge good ties with your peers. Simple courtesy can help do this.

Maintaining a Phone Number File

A phone file is a safe way of saving numbers and a fast way of retrieving them. I prefer the pop-up type that allows an alphabetical listing and retrieval of numbers. I recommend everyone maintaining a phone file (either manual or electronic) and transferring numbers and addresses into it as soon as it is reasonably likely you will need to talk to the person in the future. You will only need to do this for people not already listed in the company phone book. As most of your phone conversations will be with individuals inside the company, it will take a long time before you exhaust the capacity of a typical file.

DESK ORGANIZATION

Organizing your desk consists of doing a lot of little things. Individually they don't amount to much but collectively they can make the difference between sustained progress and chaos.

Establishing Files

A good place to start is to recognize that you will need to maintain files on your projects. A file is merely a collection of documents that pertain to a common subject. Initially, you may want to establish files on company benefits and routines. As you move into your work assignment you will want to create files and subfiles on different projects. Some of your files may reside in a computer, but you will always have need to maintain some files of paper documents. We will concentrate on the latter here.

When you start up a new file you will want to keep it initially in a hanging folder in a file drawer. As the file matures you will transfer documents out of the hanging folder into a binder. This transfer process is usually done once a year and separates working documents from ones kept for reference.

Files are usually subdivided according to category and are chronologically ordered within each subcategory. Typical subcategories are: letters of correspondence, meeting notes, project schedules, documentation, and reference material. (Notice that I didn't mention purchases. A good practice is to keep purchase orders and vouchers in separate files that consolidate all purchase orders and vouchers that you generate.) Each subproject should reside in its own folder within the hanging folder. In order to maintain the viability of the chronological ordering of your files, you will need to have a date on everything. Some items that cross your desk will have dates and some won't. A good habit is to date everything that you generate (even informal notes) and all undated items that you receive. For undated items, use the date that you receive them as the filing date. By placing new documents in the front of the file as they come in, you automatically preserve the chronological ordering.

A type of file that you don't ordinarily think about, but nevertheless is quite useful, is a business card file. Most business cards are either lost or discarded within 24 hours after they are received. A business card file is a good way of dredging up your contacts outside the company. You can buy special plastic folders that have built-in pockets for holding business cards. Before filing the card away it is a good idea to note, directly on the card, where you met the person, his or her function (titles don't usually tell you much), and the date.

Keeping a Calendar

In addition to anything you have hanging on your wall, you will need a notebook-size, folding calendar on your desk. One this size is necessary to allow you to write all of your appointments directly on the calendar. By keeping the calendar on your desk, it is readily available for your own reference and for other people's reference when you are away from your desk. (The latter aspect is important to those trying to arrange meetings that require your presence.)

Your calendar should be portable so that you can take it with you to meetings. Don't fall into the trap of trying to maintain two calendars—a stationary one for your desk and a portable one to carry with you. This practice doubles your record-ing work and allows the possibility of an event being scheduled on one calendar but not on another. For out-of-town trips you should take your calendar with you but leave duplicate copies of the current month and the next two months on your desk in its place.

Keeping a Bulletin Board

A bulletin board is a good place to post action items tem-porarily. Assignments from your boss, meeting notices, re-ceipts, and letters awaiting your reply are typical items that you might put there. This posting, along with your daily list of things to do, serves as a constant visual reminder of pending items.

One thing you should guard against is bulletin board clut-ter. Your bulletin board should not become a permanent rest-ing ground for everything. On a regular basis you should review the items on your board to determine if any should be discarded or put into more permanent files.

Avoiding Desk Congestion

I personally agree with the popular quotation that says, "A clean desk is a sign of a sick mind." I have a heck of a time keeping my desk clean. The usual cause is trying to attend to too many things at once. I end up placing action items across my desk with the intention of disposing of them before the end of the work day. (If you can pull it off without losing anything, this approach is slightly more efficient than posting or filing the items away, listing them on your things-to-do list, and retriev-ing them one at a time.) Sometimes I clear things off by the end of the day, but most times I don't. I would advise you to be bet-ter organized.

Only three legitimate types of documents belong on your desk at any one time. One is the item that you are currently working on. Another is a stack of future action items that cor-respond to the items on your things-to-do list. The last is a stack of unread memoranda and magazines. This last type is one you want to keep under control. Try to do some reading every day to avoid getting an unmanageable backlog. Reserving a portion of your workday for this purpose, say the last hour of work or immediately after work, will help you keep up.

Permanent files should not reside on your desk. It is better to spend the few minutes it takes to create an organized file than to let things just pile up.

Keeping a Working Notebook

A bound notebook helps you maintain a permanent record of assigned action items, meeting notes, and phone calls. You should write your name on its cover along with your phone number and dates that it spans. All new entries should be dated and started immediately after the last previous entry. (Although this notebook is not intended to serve as a legal document, there is always the possibility that it may be called for use as an exhibit in some case. If this happens, blank areas in the notebook could destroy its credibility.) A bound notebook is easy to carry around, is less likely to be misplaced, and avoids the possibility of losing loose pages. Because it carries all of the notes you have made in various meetings, it can be used to reference agreements, schedules, and responsibilities quickly.

Information in the bound notebook can be easily transferred to project files by photocopying the appropriate pages.

CHAPTER FOUR

SKILLS
TO ACQUIRE
Basic Tools
of a Professional

In all but the purest of technical environments, success is contingent upon an individual having nontechnical skills that complement the technical ones. These nontechnical skills may be divided into two categories—individual and interactive.

Individual skills are those that can be performed without the active involvement of others. Writing, speaking, and working efficiently fall into this category. *Interactive skills* are those used in performing tasks that require the cooperation of others. A person uses these skills whenever he or she is involved in project work, either as a leader or team member.

This chapter focuses on the tactical, as opposed to technical, aspects of implementing these skills. The technical aspects of these skills (for example, the mechanics of writing clearly and effectively) may be found in a number of other books and need not be rehashed here. Further, technical proficiency in these skills takes time to develop (be it in the classroom or on the job), and over the first few months of employment new employees will have to go with what they have at the time. On the other hand, tactics can be employed immediately. Tactics have to do with utilizing to the best advantage whatever skills a person already has.

This chapter deals with three skills that are important to initial success. The first two are individual skills: written and oral communications. The third one is interactive and deals with fostering support for your work and keeping projects on track.

WRITTEN COMMUNICATIONS: YOUR ENGLISH TEACHER WAS RIGHT

In business, written communication is a tool for establishing professional credibility. Writings may be grouped into four general categories. Each of these four types will be discussed (in order of importance) regarding their objectives and keys to success.

The Technical Memorandum

The technical memorandum is written to document the research, development, analysis, and status of projects. The keys to success center around organization, emphasis, and readability.

MEMO ORGANIZATION: THE OUTLINE

Effective writing begins with the *outline*. The outline allows you to organize your thoughts and put the work into perspective. Further, by viewing the whole paper in outline form, any holes that may exist in the work should be apparent.

The outline allows you to establish proper emphasis. Effective memoranda have messages that are clearly communicated to the reader. Establishing proper emphasis means devoting the most prominent and lengthy portions of the memo to the most important aspects of the work. For example, if a particular conclusion is important, it should not just be tacked on at the end of a summary. It should be dealt with in the heart of the memorandum, surrounded by arguments that led to the conclusion, and heralded as an important outcome of the work.

The outline is a damage-control device. To write a complete memorandum and have your boss tell you it is all wrong and needs to be rewritten is a complete waste of your time. By formulating an outline and submitting it to your boss *before* starting to write, you automatically limit the scope of any rewriting that must be done. By approving the outline, your boss gives blessing to the content, organization, and emphasis of the memorandum. Any rewriting that is called for will necessarily be restricted to items such as grammar and style.

PLACING THE EMPHASIS WHERE IT BELONGS:
NEGLECTED PARTS OF THE MEMO

The *abstract* is the one part of the memo that writers neglect the most. The abstract is usually written as an obligatory afterthought lacking both vitality and substantive information. However, the abstract is the most widely read part of the memo. (Readers usually scan the abstract to determine relevance and extract useful information, after which they either discard the memo or probe for additional information.) The abstract is the writer's first, and perhaps only, shot at the reader. Therefore, it should accurately reflect the contents of the paper and, space permitting, should state the principal results of the work.

To illustrate how seldom the entire text of a lengthy document is fully read, let me relate a true story about an experience of one of my colleagues. One of the researchers in my division was a high-powered Ph. D. who often produced great volumes of text containing analyses that were beyond the comprehension of most of his peers, let alone his managers. His findings were always advertised in his abstracts and summarized in detail in his conclusions, thus sparing the reader the burden of laboring through the entire memorandum. Nevertheless, for the sake of completeness and to permit thorough scrutiny of his work, he included his full derivations and analyses in all of his documents.

The researcher was aware of how esoteric and lengthy his memoranda were and from time to time he doubted if anyone, including his boss, ever read the whole text. One day he came up with an idea of how to test his suspicion. He decided to add a test sentence in his next memorandum. The test sentence he came up with was, "If you've read this far and are the first one to call my phone number printed on the cover sheet of this memorandum, I will send you a five dollar reward." He then added, "This offer expires sixty days after the publication date on the cover sheet." He buried these two sentences deep inside some of the text that walked the reader through his most lengthy analysis. He then let the typist know what he was doing and asked her to keep his little secret. Everything was all set.

The draft of his memorandum was approved by his supervisor without the supervisor detecting the wayward sentences. He even got a compliment on the fine job that he had done. (It was, in fact, a good piece of work.) The memorandum went out with 41 names on its distribution list. The researcher sat back and waited for the phone to ring. He waited for a week—no phone call. He called some of the people on the distribution list to see if they had received the document—no problems there. He began to wonder just how long it would take before someone discovered his little prank—he's still wondering. After three months he wasn't amused anymore and decided to clean up his document by sending out a correction sheet. The corrected sheet was identical to the original except for the removal of the two sentences that dealt with the $5.00 reward. The instructions that accompanied the sheet explained that, for the sake of clarity, some of the text had been rewritten and that the recipient should replace page 46 with the revised version. He now got a phone call. Out of curiosity, one of his peers compared the new sheet to the old and discovered the reward offer. He was surprised that he was the first to call and that no one had collected the reward. That was the only call the researcher ever received. Even though he only got one response, in due time his prank became well known—even legend.

This story emphasizes the need to get your points across in the parts of the document that are most widely read—the abstract and summary.

The section at the very end of a memorandum is usually entitled Conclusions, Summary, or Recommendations, and it is the punch line of the paper. Because its function is to put the message across, this section deserves special effort. To ensure that the message is direct and well stated, the conclusion (summary or recommendation) should be written first, when the writer is still fresh. Further, writing the conclusion first provides the writer with mental reinforcement of the focus of the memo, assists in developing supporting arguments, and helps in identifying material that must be covered before arriving at the conclusions.

References cited within the memo show that you've done your homework and are aware of previous work. *Acknowledgments* protect you from criticism from "slighted" individuals. In industry it is well known that anyone who takes credit for other people's work will burn in hell. To avoid literary damnation it is better to overextend credit than to neglect mentioning someone's contribution. Acknowledgments don't cost you anything. You may even be given more credit for mustering the support of others and coordinating their efforts than for doing all of the work yourself. Before a memo is released, you should review a checklist (which includes references, acknowledgments, and a "copy to" list) to ensure that the appropriate people and previous works are mentioned and that the right people see the document.

THE INTRODUCTION

The *introduction* should do three things. The first is to set the stage. The introduction should provide sufficient background to bring the reader up to speed as to what has gone on before. Basically, it is incumbent on the writer to establish the motivation for doing the work that is described in the memorandum.

The other two things that the introduction should do are (1) describe the objectives of the work and (2) describe the contents of the memo. The latter lets readers know what is covered (and where) without requiring them to wade through every page.

THE APPENDIX

The appendix is a parking spot for lengthy derivations, data, computer programs, and tedious analysis. It is used because the memo tends to lose focus if too much detail is placed in the body. (The main points become lost in the clutter.) Further, the more bulky the paper is, the less likely it is to be read. The appendix addresses these problems without omitting details that may be important to some individuals.

READABILITY (PARAGRAPH CONSTRUCTION)

It is not the intent of this author to get into grammatical rules and the mechanics of good writing. However, one fault will be mentioned here because of its prevalence and power of destruction. The culprit is the rambling paragraph.

The first (or second) sentence of a paragraph should express the central theme. Other sentences should support the first one. A paragraph that contains several disjointed thoughts leaves the reader wondering just what was the point the paragraph was trying to make.

The rambling paragraph reflects lack of organization (usually caused by not working from an outline). When your manager reviews your memorandum before its publication, reorganization of sentences and paragraphs into logical groupings is a big undertaking that the manager usually does not have time to do. Instead, you will more likely be asked to do a total rewrite of the paper. This disaster can be avoided by checking to see that thoughts are logically grouped within the outline.

WRITING TIPS

It has been said that "there is no good writing, only good rewriting." Errors and awkward expressions are easier to spot the second time around. First, get it down on paper (or in your word processor), let it get cold (for at least a day), then rewrite it. Another thing that is helpful is to have another person look it over if you can find someone willing to devote the time to do it. A peer review of your draft document often provides feedback you are happier to get than that coming from your boss.

There are a number of excellent books on writing. Three that the author recommends are *Elements of Style*, by Strunk and White (1979); *Handbook of Technical Writing*, by Brusaw, Alred, and Oliu (1982); and *Art of Readable Writing*, by R. Flesch (1984).

Meeting Notes

Meeting notes are written to document, as factually as possible, just what took place during a meeting. (I'm willing to take some flak on this point. Some crafty veterans will tell you that as long as you are stuck with the job of writing the meeting notes, that you might as well be a bit selective in what you record and bias things to favor your point of view. This is dangerous and can cause you loss of credibility.) The two principal objectives of this type of documentation are (1) to serve as a vehicle for getting things done, and (2) to record meeting activities for nonattenders. The keys to success are timeliness, completeness, accuracy, and proper distribution.

TIMELINESS

News loses its value more rapidly than unrefrigerated fish. Each day that meeting notes are delayed in getting out diminishes their impact. Timely notes are more appreciated because of their relevance, and because the grapevine has had less chance to steal their thunder.

People are more forgiving of notes that are hot off the press. They tend to be less critical of style and grammar when it is clear that the news has been rushed to their hands. Thus, rapid publication takes some of the pressure off the writer.

Memory fades with time. The earlier that notes are written, the better chance they have of (1) accurately reflecting what took place and (2) being complete.

Meeting notes that come out too late will be ineffective in performing one of their principal objectives—to *lead* action. Meeting notes should advertise and thus precede any action they describe as forthcoming.

Finally, prompt meeting notes help build the writer's image of being a rapid mover who is self-motivated and highly capable.

COMPLETENESS

Meeting notes should be concise yet complete. They should be no more elaborate than is necessary to cover the three fundamental points: (1) statement of meeting purpose, (2) documentation of what took place, and (3) summary of agreements, action items, responsibilities, and scheduled future meetings.

ACCURACY

On occasion it may be necessary to solicit comments on a draft before releasing the notes. The official reason for soliciting comments is to ensure accuracy but usually such precautions are taken for political reasons or if major commitments were made. Soliciting comments should only be done when absolutely necessary. Giving others a shot at a draft helps avoid criticism, but delays publication. If comments are solicited, a deadline should be given for getting input back to the writer.

DISTRIBUTION LIST

People who should receive the meeting notes are those who signed the attendance list; those who are regular members of the group but were not present at this particular meeting; and those who have action responsibilities, their bosses, and your boss.

Letters of Correspondence

Letters of correspondence are generally exchanged with customers, suppliers, and internal organizations, and their objectives may be to request action, document agreements, establish policy, summarize status, or transfer data. The keys to effective letters of correspondence are providing sufficient information to make them understandable and being direct as possible without being rude (clarity).

SUFFICIENT INFORMATION

Letters are often written by subordinates for their boss's signature. Managers (and others not intimately involved with the details of a project) may have a hard time understanding the motivation for a letter (or even what's being asked for) without sufficient information or a point of reference. In order to provide such background without insulting the addressee, you can use phrases like, "As you recall. . .," or "Reviewing the project status to date. . . ." When a letter is written as a reply, it may be sufficient just to begin with, "This is in response to your letter dated. . . requesting (or in which you stated). . . ."

CLARITY

The writer should focus on clarity. Simple, direct statements are preferable to flowery ones. When referring to items that have code designations (such as 710 Connector) it is a good practice to refer to the item by its descriptive or functional title followed by the code designation in parentheses. For example, "My question concerns the 25-pair wire connector (710 Connector)."

People often write strong letters, clearly establishing their point, but conclude with vague statements that let the other party off the hook. For example, ". . . therefore work must start on this project soon," or ". . . please let me know how you feel about this proposal," or ". . . please give this matter your most urgent consideration." None of the above requests definitively specifies time frames. Sometimes you can't afford to be pushy, but you can be definitive. For example, a call for action might read, ". . . our project schedule is such that your assistance would benefit us most if you could complete this work within six weeks," or "If you concur with this proposal, I would like for the project to get started immediately and aim for a completion date of March 1, this year." Be clear in what you want and when you need it.

Informal Documents

The objective of informal, sometimes handwritten, notes is quick correspondence. By the very nature of these, little is demanded regarding style and form. There are, however, a few commonsense things to remember. First, take the time to make all notes legible. Date them. Make sure the right people either get copies or are on the circulation list. (The "right people" are those who might have a direct interest in the matter under consideration.)

Sometimes notes are written on slips that are paper-clipped to documents. Aside from providing routing information, these slips allow "margin notes" to be made without writing directly on the document. Notes made in this way provide a trail of comments from the various handlers of the document.

A new type of informal communications has emerged via internal mail networks. This is a powerful channel for speeding communications. This method is only slightly more formal than a telephone conversation, but you nevertheless should make sure that copies of the correspondence are routed to the proper people.

ORAL COMMUNICATIONS: YOUR CREDIBILITY IS ON THE LINE

Thus far we have only talked about written communications. We will now switch gears and discuss the much more dynamic and influential form of communication—oral communication.

Many people (especially managers) form their opinion of you based on your oral technical presentations. Accordingly, crisp, well-organized presentations that get their point across can help you more than anything else that you do. The converse is also true. In this section a few tips are offered on how to organize and carry out presentations to maximize your chances of success.

The Truth About Oral Communications

The term *oral communication* is a misnomer. Studies done to assess the impact of speeches on audiences show that the visual component of a speech accounts for 55 percent of the impact, the vocal component (the speaker's tone, clarity, and fluency) accounts for 37 percent, and the verbal component (what was actually said) accounts for only 8 percent. Thus, the nonverbal portion of a message has an impact that is roughly ten times greater than the verbal portion. Blasphemy, you say! Does this mean that form is more important than substance? Absolutely not. It is just that other things that you do may be more instrumental in communicating the message than what you actually say. The value of an oral presentation is the coherence that the speaker brings to the subject matter. What members of the audience see helps fix the message in their memories, and how the message is delivered affects its credibility.

Preparation: Choosing the Format and Means of Delivery

Don't memorize everything. The less material you memorize, the less the danger of forgetting something. Instead of memorizing specific *sentences,* mentally formulate the *messages* that you want to get across. Your talks will appear more natural and you will be able to handle interruptions more gracefully if you are not constrained to follow a written or memorized script.

Whenever possible, structure your talk around transparencies. Transparencies do wonders for a speaker. They provide the speaker with a crutch that minimizes the need to memorize material. The outline of the talk can actually be embedded in the transparency. (*Caution:* It is bad form simply to read your talk from what is projected on the screen.) Other prompts can be written as margin notes on the transparencies' frames.

If you are shy, visual aids like transparencies can help make you invisible. When visual material is presented, the attention of the audience tends to be diverted toward the screen and away from the speaker. In this sense, transparencies are the next best thing to a lectern to hide behind.

Provided that they are not overdone, transparencies make a presentation appear more spontaneous and less staged than do slides. Portions of the foil may also be selectively exposed as the speaker works through a particular point.

Transparencies are also flexible. They can be written on and can be updated more easily than slides. Attention can be focused from one item to another on the same transparency by moving a pointer (like a pencil) around the projector table. The use of multiple overlays, repeat use of transparencies (at different points in the talk), and the freedom of interchanging their sequence at will are all part of transparencies' flexibility. Foils can also be photocopied to provide your audience with hard copies of your talk. Finally, there is no mechanical apparatus to go awry.

A caution about all visual aids: They can be overdone. To guard against overuse, for each visual aid that you plan to use, ask yourself these questions: "What contribution does this item make?" "How does it support the message that's being delivered?" "Is it needed?"

Talks are opportunities to create impressions on the audience. To take advantage of this to the fullest, the speaker should formulate a clear message that he or she wants to get across. One should be able to write out, in a sentence or two, what the message is that one wants the audience to come away with. Going through such an exercise will make it easier to construct the talk and help ensure that the emphasis is in the right places. Speakers may choose to conclude their talks with an explicit statement of the message.

Often the message is embedded in one's body English. For example, although a presentation may deal with design (or performance) details of a new product, the *message* may be that this new product is far better than anything else on the market. Or a financial status report may portray dwindling revenues but have a message that decisive action needs to be taken immediately in order to turn things around. It is up to the speaker to clearly separate, in the speaker's own mind, the message from the topic.

While in the preparation stage, the speaker should ensure that the level of the presentation is matched to the audience. This usually requires that the speaker seek out information on the background and composition of the audience. Things like job level, function, and years of experience are relevant factors.

Execution: Organization and Tactics

No attempt is made here to deal with the mechanics or style of delivering a presentation. Instead, several points are emphasized regarding organization.

Spend some time setting the stage. Bring the audience up to a common level by providing sufficient background on the topic. By doing this you retain a larger percentage of your audience for a longer period of time and you avoid putting some individuals in the embarrassing position of having to ask questions that reveal their lack of knowledge.

Let members of your audience know up front what the format of the presentation will be. If you wish to handle questions in real time (that is, allow interruptions), let them know it is okay. If you have structured your talk otherwise, you should let them know that, too. If you will be giving a demonstration, let them know it is coming and what it will illustrate. If the talk is a lengthy one (over 30 minutes), it is good practice to let the audience know how you have structured the talk and what subtopics will be covered.

All of the above practices serve a function in addition to the ones mentioned. They help stall for comfort and attention. Audience members need time to get comfortable with the speaker before they can devote full attention to what is being said. During the first few moments the audience is sizing up the speaker—taking note of personal details that have nothing to do with the talk. For the most part the audience is only half listening. To get through this warm-up period some speakers start off with a joke or funny story. This works great when they can pull it off. It is not, however, always easy to do (or appropriate), and when it doesn't work it is embarrassing for both speaker and audience, making a tense situation worse. The low-keyed, stage-setting items mentioned in the preceding paragraph are safe, methodical ways of getting through the warm-up phase.

Damage-control mechanisms are needed when handling questions from the audience. Loss of rapport is a major disaster that can take place when the audience senses the speaker is bluffing or not responding to questions. The latter problem can be avoided by making it a standard practice to repeat all questions asked from the floor. What this does is to (1) guarantee that you understand the question well enough to paraphrase it, (2) assure that everyone has heard the question, and (3) provide you with a bit of extra time to formulate a response.

Bluffing to conceal ignorance is dangerous and can quickly lead to loss of credibility. When unsure of an answer it is best to admit your uncertainty and immediately follow with ". . . let me find the answer and get back to you."

The ending is the part of the presentation that is most often not thought out well enough. If unplanned, it can be abrupt and catch the audience by surprise. To ease the audience into the ending you might use phrases like ". . . my last two transparencies show. . ." or "There's one other point I'd like to make before I wrap up" or "Tying everything together. . . ." Once you have gotten the audience prepped for the ending, take advantage of this opportunity to underscore your main points or emphasize your message. Your concluding sentences might be along the lines of: "In summary. . ." or "Let me conclude with. . ." or ". . . and finally, the message I want to leave with you is. . . ." The key is not how the ending is carried out (its style), but that it be planned.

In summary, the principal points of this section are:

1. Let the audience know what you will cover.

2. Cover it.

3. Summarize it

EFFECTIVE WORK SKILLS: GETTING IT
TOGETHER TO RUN A TIGHT SHIP
AND EXHIBIT UNCOMMON PROFESSIONALISM

This section deals with cultivating personal characteristics and work routines that pave the way for success in the corporate environment. Successful individuals tend to be assertive, well-organized people who get results. They usually show sound judgment and have the ability to get others involved in supporting their work. These traits can be developed. As will be shown, such characteristics are just the outward signs that these individuals are employing effective problem-solving techniques. Much of the advice offered in this section deals with having you ask yourself the right questions.

Organize to Meet Commitments:
Heading-Off Those Reasons
for Failure

Meeting commitments means not only doing everything that you promised you would but also doing it *on time*. The ability to keep projects on schedule can be improved by being aware of the principal reasons for schedule slips and practicing routines that avoid these pitfalls. Such reasons include: (1) faulty planning, (2) important items going undone, (3) critical subtasks taking longer than expected, (4) failure of support people, (5) insufficient resources, and (6) plain old bad judgment. The last two items will be dealt with as separate topics in the two sections that follow. The others are discussed below.

FAULTY PLANNING

Careful planning at the onset of a project can avoid crises later on. If services are needed from support organizations (drafting, marketing, data processing, library, purchasing, etc.), the lead time that they require should be factored into the schedule. If special, heroic efforts are needed from support organizations, then these organizations should be consulted to see if the impossible is, in fact, possible and if they are willing to make the effort. (A word of caution: Your credibility can be lost along with your ability to get rush jobs done in the future if you overstate the urgency of your request. Don't say you need it tomorrow if next week is soon enough. Furthermore, on all rush jobs, personally pick them up as soon as you are notified that they are ready.)

IMPORTANT ITEMS REMAINING UNDONE

Tasks should not just "fall through the crack." Writing down a daily list of "Things to Do" helps guard against items being forgotten. Further, by listing the items in order of priority and attacking the most urgent items first, you can better assure that you will keep on schedule. Jobs that aren't finished one day should be carried over to the next day's list. The list should be kept on your desk or in some other conspicuous place to serve as a constant visual reminder.

A task is said to be on the "critical path" of a project schedule if the total time it takes to complete it and other tasks that must be done in *series* with it takes longer than any other series of operations associated with the project. In other words, the critical path begins at the project start date, ends at the project end date, and traces through the longest chronological sequence of tasks. Any slips that occur on items on the critical path will cause the entire project completion date to be delayed. By first identifying the critical path in the schedule and then riding close herd on items along that path, one can do a better job of keeping a project on schedule.

CRITICAL SUBTASKS TAKING LONGER THAN
EXPECTED

It is also important to keep work going on items not on the critical path. It is entirely possible to have sufficient slips to change noncritical items into critical ones. They now become a part of the new critical path. To avoid this you should make a habit of pushing secondary tasks along while awaiting the completion of primary jobs. To guarantee that no secondary items are forgotten, ask yourself, "What would I still have to do if the task that I'm waiting for others to complete were complete today?" (Some examples: If the computer simulation and drafting work were finished today, would the project be finished or would you still have to get started on the write-up? If the testing machine that's on order arrived today could you start testing right away or would you first have to prepare test samples or test fixtures?) Answering this question assures that those parts of a project that can be kept moving will, in fact, be kept moving.

FAILURE OF SUPPORT PEOPLE

A show of interest on your part can reduce the likelihood of a schedule being wrecked by failure of support people. When you can do it without ruffling too many feathers, it is a good idea to check periodically on the status of work being done for you by others. In addition to keeping you alerted to possible problems, this reinforces to the other party that this job is important. The further out the scheduled completion date is, the more the need for this type of follow-up. Don't wait until the last week of a six-month project to check the status. Check it after one week just to ensure that it has been started and not been bumped by someone else's hot project. Check at other times to afford the supplier opportunities to ask questions and make suggestions.

Be Resourceful: Find a Way to Get It Done

Being resourceful means accentuating the positive. It means finding a way to get the job done with what is available.

In one sense being resourceful means having the ability to gather sufficient resources to carry out your work. The scarcest and most valuable resource is not money but people's time. It thus follows that a valuable skill in industry is the ability to get support from others in carrying out your work. This is never an easy task and cannot be treated casually. Even managers must be persuasive when handing out job assignments if they are to get subordinates to respond enthusiastically and put forth a high-quality effort.

Situations always arise where cooperation from peers and other organizations is needed to carry out projects. To consistently get such cooperation you need an arsenal of tools, including charm (when it will work), bargaining skill, and political adroitness. Whatever the approach, the structure of the solicitation remains the same. The four components are summarized below:

1. Call for help

2. Explanation of need and priority (information sharing)

3. Inducement (negotiation)

4. Closure.

The four components are nearly self-explanatory. The *call for help* sets the tone of the conversation and should acknowledge the dependency of the party requesting support. A perfectly good statement is, "Bill, I need your help." The *explanation* step is basically one of information sharing. It puts the request in context, establishes why the request is being made, and defines its urgency (priority). The *inducement* stage establishes the incentive for the support organization or individual to do the work. This is where bargaining, charm, and other selling approaches are employed. During *closure* the agreement is finalized and completion dates are agreed upon. Remember: *Any request that fails to specify a completion date is frivolous* and is likely to be treated as such; that is, it won't be fulfilled.

Being resourceful sometimes means finding alternate ways of getting a job done. Situations often arise where you find yourself dependent on a single means for doing a particular job (single-source supplier). Should this source fail, or be late in delivery, an entire project may be jeopardized. For this reason it is smart to have alternate sources for critical items. To help you identify alternate sources, a good question to ask is, "How would I do this job if the primary source of help didn't exist?" The answer to this question will not only point the way to other solutions but will also provide a calibration on how effective (as far as cost and time) the primary approach is. In addition to these benefits, you are in a better position to answer the question that management always asks: "Have you considered other ways of doing this?"

Cultivate Good Judgment: It's a Learnable Skill

An employee who takes a business trip when a phone call will accomplish the same purpose is showing bad judgment. Employees who devote so much time to nontechnical activities that their technical performance is noticeably affected are showing bad judgment. A person who overspends on a piece of equipment or supplies when less expensive items will work just as well is showing poor judgment. A person who makes a crucial project decision without soliciting appropriate input from key individuals or organizations is showing poor judgment. (A point of clarification: Bad judgment should not be confused with dishonest or illegal acts. Bad judgment refers to taking action that does not violate any established rules but nevertheless is a poor choice in the light of other available alternatives.) These examples of bad judgment are easy to recognize, but what exactly constitutes good judgment? Furthermore, why is good judgment so important and how do you acquire it?

Good judgment is an often used, yet nebulous, term that refers to one's overall ability to make rational decisions with, or without, a complete set of information. More specifically, it is the ability to select from a collection of options some particular course that has a reasonable probability of achieving the desired result with a minimum of undesirable side effects.

Your judgment, good or bad, affects your manager's confidence in you. It doesn't matter how competent you are in your special field of training, if you are pegged as having bad judgment, you won't be trusted with much responsibility. And therein lies its importance. Bad judgment can undo all the good things that you accomplish through your regular job effort. Without the confidence of your manager, your chances of success are practically nil.

For those of you who have self-doubts about your sense of good judgment, despair not. Techniques are available for developing good judgment on the types of issues commonly dealt with in the workplace. There are four fundamental elements of good judgment, namely: (1) foresight, (2) sense of perspective,

(3) sense of propriety, and (4) sense of economy. In this section we will look at each of these traits and offer suggestions for nurturing their development.

FORESIGHT

Foresight is really forethought. It is not that some people have the ability to see into the future better than the rest of us, but rather that some people take the time to contemplate various scenarios for achieving their goal prior to taking action. We all could be more productive if we stopped to consider the repercussions of our actions before we put them in motion. For example, it is easier to gain the cooperation of another individual if you first put yourself in that person's shoes, look at your request from his or her point of view, and formulate an approach that stands a reasonable chance of success before making that first contact. As another example, before sending off a heated letter calling for action, it is wise to reflect back on the outcome that you wish to achieve. You might ask yourself: How will others react to this letter? Will this letter make things better or worse? Would another approach be more effective? Is a letter needed at all? The key here is to present yourself with options and examine the consequences of each option. In making a choice, two things should be kept in mind. The option chosen should (1) have a realistic chance of success, and (2) not have long-term effects that might diminish your effectiveness on the job; that is, permanently damage relations with others, reduce your credibility, or narrow your career options.

The best foresight comes from hindsight. It is difficult for an inexperienced employee to look down the road at the start of a project, anticipate all the things that can go wrong, and make plans to guard against such occurrences. Also, without experience it is difficult to come up with realistic time and cost estimates for performing specific tasks. Here is where hindsight comes in. In all likelihood, somebody else in your company has had to make plans for a similar project. In fact, someone had to do the same job that you have been assigned, for whatever system or program that preceded the one that you are currently working on. Find that person, or someone with similar experience, and get that person to comment on your project plans. In most cases he or she will be able to identify issues you never would have thought about on your own. The message is clear:

Don't be afraid of asking for help or soliciting the opinions of experienced people—they will be flattered. The best advice comes from someone who has been there.

SENSE OF PERSPECTIVE

Having a sense of perspective means keeping in mind the overall objective when planning and carrying out your work. In some cases this may mean taking care to distribute your energies among various tasks in a manner consistent with their importance to the success of the project. In every case it means keeping sight of the end objective and making sure that your work stays on a path that leads to that target.

SENSE OF PROPRIETY

Having a sense of propriety means being in tune with accepted norms. Stated another way, it means acting in a manner appropriate to the situation. This pertains to conduct regarding personal items (such as choice of clothes, language, and topics of conversation) as well as business conduct.

In a business situation the classic example of poor sense of propriety is conflict of interest. The media are replete with stories about individuals taking advantage of their position in a company to gain unfair personal benefits for themselves, relatives, or friends. A simple way to test your sense of propriety on any issue is to ask yourself: Is it legal? Is it honest? Is it fair? Will it help the company's image? Would it be all right if everybody did it? If the answer is no to any of these questions, it shouldn't be done.

SENSE OF ECONOMY

The best way to guide your judgments on questions of economy is to ask yourself three sets of questions. The first set guards against overspending, the second set guards against underspending, and the third set addresses risk management. There are two questions related to *overspending*: (1) Would I make this purchase if I were spending my own money? and (2) Am I getting this item at a fair price? (in comparison to what other suppliers quote for similar items). Answering the first question requires you to do some sort of cost-benefit analysis, whereas answering the second requires you to look at other products and suppliers. Just thinking of purchases in these terms automatically puts you on the right track.

In some situations, *underspending* can be more disastrous than overspending. This is true when first cost is not the only issue surrounding a purchase. Other issues may be (1) operating and maintenance costs, (2) product reliability, and (3) dependability of supplier. These three issues should be looked at when a quoted price is unbelievably low and way out of line with the competition. You should then ask the following: How do operating and maintenance costs affect the total cost of using this particular product? What are the consequences of the product breaking down while in service? How dependable is the supplier with regard to meeting delivery schedules, standing behind the product (assuming financial responsibility), and servicing the product?

Risk management involves hedging your bet to soften the downside risk. In the case of purchased products, the principal risk is not being able to obtain delivery on a workable product in the time frame needed. The relevant questions then become: (1) What are the quoted delivery intervals for the item? and (2) How important is the item to the overall success of the project in which it will be used? If the advertised interval between order time and product delivery is excessively long and would affect the project schedule, the purchaser must make a decision to: (1) negotiate an earlier delivery date, (2) order from another supplier (who may advertise a shorter interval but may not be as good on, say, dependability), or (3) extend the project schedule. If time is the dominant issue, you might have to pursue both options (1) and (2) simultaneously. In both cases, special action is required to ensure timely product delivery. For negotiated short-delivery dates the purchaser should pay a premium and should make on-time delivery a condition of payment. For alternate, short-interval suppliers, the purchaser should meet with them to emphasize the importance of the delivery date, ensure that there is no misunderstanding as to what is being asked for, and to make certain that the supplier has the capability to deliver on time.

Sometimes the situation may be that, although it is too early in a project to determine if a particular item will be needed, the product delivery interval is so long that the item must be ordered at once in order for it to arrive on time if needed. In such cases you can look at the price of the item as a premium paid to help ensure meeting the project deadline. With that point of view you can make the decision as to whether the additional assurance of meeting the product deadline warrants the expense (balance of risks). Finally, for those cases where an item is absolutely essential for the project's success and time is not an issue, it is often best to pay a higher price than you would like initially and plan for a cost-reduction program later on.

CHAPTER FIVE

THINGS TO DO

**Suggestions
on Personal Conduct
and
Interpersonal Interactions**

The two previous chapters dealt with absorbing information and developing skills to enhance chances of early success. Both of these processes—learning and skill development—take time. There are, however, some things that can and should be done from day one. The performance of an employee in such areas strongly influences management's first impressions, establishes the working climate with fellow employees, and influences the direction of one's professional growth. This chapter deals with those things that a new employee should take pains to do and do well.

TECHNICAL BEHAVIOR

By technical behavior is meant how an employee performs in carrying out tasks that require special skill or training. There are two issues. One is how well a new employee does the job he or she was hired to do. The other is whether the employee exhibits those characteristics that will make the person a valuable employee in the future. The first three items discussed in this section address the initial performance issue, whereas the last three address growth and potential.

Quick Start

The following words of wisdom come from many seasons of coaching basketball: *You can't win a basketball game in the first half, but you sure can lose it.* Deep holes are hard to climb out of. Furthermore, a poor start is psychologically bad in that it can plant seeds of doubt and cause you to waste time looking back at the past instead of focusing on present and future challenges.

Get off to a good start. The time for celebration and relaxation is over. Although you may feel that you deserve a break after working all those years to get your new position, you can't afford to slow down now. If you feel burnt out and need to recuperate, then take a vacation before you report to work. Don't look forward to resting on the job. When you report to your new job, you must be mentally and physically prepared to give a maximum effort for a sustained period of time.

Regardless of how good your credentials are, people are skeptical until they see for themselves how you perform. Essentially you must prove yourself all over again. This is a challenge and an opportunity. It is a challenge and a test of your maturity for you to dig down and muster the effort required to build a reputation from scratch. At the same time it is an opportunity to show that you are, in fact, as good as or better than what you looked like on paper, and that you have the energy and initiative that the company needs.

If you ever intend to work hard on your job, now is the time to do it because this is the time when you can get the best return on your investment. First of all, you always want a good effort to be noticed. During the first few months on the job, new employees are given greater than average attention. This is then your window of opportunity. Perform well while you are in the spotlight rather than waiting until you are off stage.

Looking at return on investment in a second way, it is clear that it takes much more effort and time to establish a good reputation if you get off to a slow start. In such cases, in order to convince people that their initial calibration of you was incorrect, you must not only make a turnaround to balance out the poor effort, but you must also now sustain that performance for an extended period in order to convince people that what they are seeing is the real you. Assuming that the slump, turnaround, and recovery periods all take about the same amount of time, this adds up to taking three times as long to establish a good image with a poor start as it does with a good start. But even heroic, come-from-behind efforts might not be enough to erase long-lasting effects of a poor start. For example, during your slump and rebuilding periods the company may have conducted performance appraisals. Your salary may thus have been negatively affected in a way that might take years to recover from. But even in those fortunate cases where salaries are not affected, visions of early subpar performances tend to linger in managers' minds and have a way of migrating to their gut. Managers are well known for relying on their gut feelings.

Another reason for getting off to a quick start is to preserve your career-development options. Elizabeth Rosen, a technical staffing specialist at AT&T Bell Laboratories, has developed a model that shows how career-development options diminish with declining performance. An adaptation of this model is illustrated in Figure 2 on page 92. The first column lists possible components of a career-development plan. The remaining columns divide the work population into four performance categories: Star Performers, Solid Citizens, Marginal Performers, and Problem Performers. The bulleted items indicate which courses of action are appropriate for each performance category.

Because they have peer support and management's confidence, Star Performers are often given considerable latitude in maintaining and developing their professional skills. Because these individuals have track records of consistently putting forth high-quality efforts, management is usually confident that almost any activity that such a Star Performer might get involved in will be productive for the company. Thus, usually the only constraint is that the activity be affordable and have a reasonable potential for returning something of value to the business unit. For Star Performers, all doors are open. Their only career-development issues are to maintain momentum and seize the initiative when opportunities arise.

Solid Citizens also have viable options for career development, but they are not as broad. Promotion may not be an op-

Options of a Career Action Plan	Employees Categorized by Performance Level			
	Star Performers	Solid Citizens	Marginal Performers	Problem Performers
• Promotion	•			
• Leadership Development				
—Special Assignment or Appointment	•	•		
—Special Training	•	•		
• Broaden Skill Base				
—Internship	•	•		
—Additional Education (Company or Univ.)	•	•	•	
—Change in Assignment	•	•	•	
• Redesign Current Job				
—Increase Responsibility	•			
—Change in Role	•		•	•
—Change in Focus (Product or Customer)	•		•	•
• Intercompany Transfer	•	•	•	•
• Outplacement				•

FIGURE 2 Career coaching model.
Adapted from E. A. Rosen's *Career Coaching Intervention Model. Putting It All Together: Working Toward Career Satisfaction* (Short Hills, NJ: AT&T Bell Laboratories, 1985).

tion and job redesign tends to be limited to just a change in role or focus. The same degree of confidence factor that enables management to feel comfortable in relinquishing the control that goes along with handing over greater responsibility is not present. Similarly, in the skill-broadening area, management tends to be more conservative in the type of projects that it will approve and the amount of resources it is willing to commit. Although all facets of skill broadening are still possible, there tend to be fewer opportunities, and management likes to have more solid economic justification for whatever action is taken.

For employees having performance standings below the first two levels, some erosion of competence has already taken place. Thus, career-development options are even more narrow. For these employees the focus moves from maintenance and development to intervention and salvage. The promotion and leadership-development options completely drop off. In their place emerge other options such as intercompany transfer.

(The intent of such transfers is to place individuals in a job that better matches up with their skills and interests as opposed to unloading a subpar performer onto some other organization.) The options that remain in both the skill-broadening and job-redesign arenas are more limited. Finally, for Problem Performers, career development has a very restrictive meaning. Management has given up on improving the employee's ability to handle the present job, and the only remaining options are intercompany transfer or outplacement. You never want your job performance to deteriorate this far. Again, in order to preserve your development options, it is to your advantage to get yourself seeded as high on the performance ladder as possible early in your career and to strive to sustain that ranking.

Finally, it is just more efficient to start quickly. On every job there are special routines or technical aspects that must be learned before a new person can become fully proficient. It makes more sense to learn such things early and minimize the length of time you spend operating from a disadvantaged position.

Positive Attitude

You want to reflect a positive attitude toward the company and your job. In order for new employees to be accepted by their co-workers, they must first accept the company. They must embrace the company as *their* company and not just an outfit that they happen to be working for at the time. They must personally "buy in" to the company's culture and corporate objectives. This buy-in is also necessary before individuals can fully commit themselves to the company. Such a commitment is what all companies look for in choosing future leaders.

No one likes being around a grouch or habitual complainer. The impact that these people have on an organization is to lower morale and distract it from the business at hand. The prevailing attitude is that grumblers can make better use of their energies by either actively working to improve whatever situation they are in or by seeking employment elsewhere.

Ownership

Ownership means taking responsibility for and being committed to your work. Even when you must depend on others, you must shoulder the ultimate responsibility.

You will be held accountable for your work's accuracy and for getting it in on time. Any input that others provide should be checked for consistency and to ensure that facts can be traced to their source. You can protect yourself from late deliveries by: (1) negotiating firm and specific delivery dates, (2) making sure that those commitments are well advertised, and (3) conducting frequent status checks without making a nuisance of yourself.

Being committed means: (1) holding a firm belief that the ultimate outcome will be positive, (2) devoting whatever energies necessary to assure a positive outcome, and (3) accepting personal responsibility. An example that illustrates the consequences of lack of commitment is the story of a man and his tomato garden.

Although his wife had planted the seeds, the man was not convinced that the soil was fertile enough to grow vegetables (lack of belief). Consequently, he saw no reason to water it regularly (withheld resources and energy) and the garden failed. He didn't feel at fault (lack of personal responsibility) because, after all, he had said from the beginning that the soil was too poor to grow anything.

Thus, a lack of commitment can set you up for failure through the scenario of the self-fulfilling prophesy. (As a side comment, the wife probably could have gotten more commitment out of her husband if she had gotten him to help her plant the seeds as opposed to planting them all herself.)

What you want to keep in mind is that you don't want to just go through the motions; but rather through aggressiveness, personal commitment, and faith (yes, faith), get the job done.

Technical Knowledge

Keep your technical knowledge up-to-date. In any profession there are two types of technical information. The first is general knowledge that is circulated publicly. The second is knowledge that is circulated inside the company and usually pertains to specific projects or products. You need to stay on top of both. With regard to public knowledge, you should allocate some portion of your time to scanning trade journals, reading articles in technical publications, and, on occasion, attending professional seminars or conferences. Internal knowledge includes current project schedules, product names, capabilities, costs, current corporate strategy, priorities, and upcoming projects. Such knowledge is maintained by doing a thorough job of reviewing relevant documents that are routed past your desk, attending meetings, and being alert in your everyday conversations. Maintaining a good storehouse of internal knowledge helps build a sharp image.

Professional Growth

Develop and expand your work skills to take more professional responsibility. Young employees typically get raises that are much better than employees who are mature in their level. There are two reasons for this. First, because younger employees are more mobile and marketable, companies must pay more to keep them. The second is that during their first few years with the company they are on the steep portion of the learning curve. It is *expected* that every year they will get more efficient at their job and they will increase the number of things that they can do.

People can increase their work skills by taking university courses, short courses offered by vendors, company courses, and through special job assignments. New employees should be alert for such opportunities and take advantage of them to the extent that they do not detract from their performance on their primary job.

Working Fertile Ground

Get some responsibility for some part of an "important" project. Don't be fooled. Just because you have been working hard and producing excellent results doesn't mean that you will be properly rewarded. You need two other things—visibility and job continuity. Both of these can be provided by an assignment to an important project.

What's an important project? You don't need an official company report to answer that question. Which projects seem to dominate the lunch table conversation? Which projects garner the most attention from management? Which projects have the most and best people assigned to them? Which projects are discussed in company announcements? These are the "important" projects.

Since, by definition, management is closely involved in important projects, such projects afford natural opportunities to showcase your talent. Hot projects are usually technically challenging and thus help you maintain your technical acuity. And because hot projects generally involve new products or services, they tend to have good life expectancy and good growth potential. Both of these last two items are important for job continuity.

Finally, rapid technological advances and spectacular results are more likely to occur on relatively new projects (which hot projects tend to be). Thus, the ground is potentially more fertile on hot projects, but, of course, the potential for failure is also greater.

Special Considerations for Continuous Process Work

Most of the advice presented in this text applies equally well to continuous process work as to project work. (Continuous process work is that involving an ongoing operation that produces a more or less continuous output such as manufacturing, sales, and most service jobs.) There are, however, fundamental differences in focus of these two types of work, which in turn drive people working in these areas to put their emphasis in different places. For example, in project work the three principal measures of success of the project are: (1) Did the product meet its cost and performance objectives?, (2) Was the project completed on time and within the allotted development budget?, and (3) Did the product sell? On the other hand, in continuous process work the principal measures of performance are: (1) How productive or efficient was the operation?, (2) How well were ship (or delivery) dates met?, (3)

How well were cost objectives met?, (4) How effectively were new projects handled?, and (5) Was the customer satisfied? The last three items in the continuous process list pretty much overlap items on the project list. However, even with this overlap, these issues tend to be attacked differently. This section explores the differences between project work and continuous process work and provides advice that is tailored specifically for the latter.

One of the things that struck me when I first started watching baseball games as a child was the enormous amount of statistics kept on every aspect of the game. There were not only batting averages for each player, but statistics on RBI (runs batted in), on-base percentage, earned-run average, number of strikeouts, walks, errors, batting average with runners in scoring position (which always seemed to me to be a particularly cruel statistic, one that measured a batter's tendency to choke in the clutch), strikeout percentage, stolen bases, wild pitches, passed balls, double plays, slugging percentage, and on and on and on—even an array of statistics on crowd size.

In contrast, very few statistics seemed to be kept in, say, auto racing or horse racing. The focus seemed to be on which combination of driver, horse (or horsepower), and preparation would prevail on a particular course on a particular day. This analogy underscores the differences in focus of project work and continuous process work. In continuous process work, as in baseball, the operations are repetitive and lend themselves to statistical analysis. Furthermore, wins in both situations tend to be by narrow margins and it pays to be able to play the odds. Thus, it is not that baseball folk have an inbred proclivity for statistics, but that the process lends itself to the accumulation of statistics that, when properly analyzed and utilized, can provide a winning edge.

On the other hand, in auto racing, as in project work, the fewer number of events and greater variety between them make it difficult to assemble more than a handful of meaningful statistics. It is hard to read trends when you have only about a dozen Indianapolis-type car races a year, run on different tracks and different conditions. Though some common features always exist, every project seems to be unique. Thus, the use of statistics and controls tend to be subordinated.

Measures of Success
for Continuous Process
Work

The remainder of this section focuses on the five principal measures of success for continuous process operations. The first performance measure is productivity and/or efficiency.

PRODUCTIVITY

Productivity is measured by the rate at which a product of acceptable quality is cranked through the process. By its very nature, continuous process work is process intensive; that is, it involves repetitive operations that act on either materials or information (data). Thus, whether you are involved in a manufacturing operation or a staff support activity, it is important for you to be thoroughly familiar with the mechanics of the process and the substance of the routines for these are core elements of the business. Knowledge of the process allows you to understand what factors in the operation limit productivity and where attention should be directed to make improvements. It also allows you to be able to talk on a nuts and bolts level to people in the business and thereby increase your technical credibility.

The focus on productivity naturally leads to a search for controls and automation. The net output of a continuous process operation can be either a manufactured product or a written document. In either case the product must conform to some predetermined standard. Organizations involved in continuous process operations usually devise a system of controls as one means of assuring that their output conforms to agreed-upon standards. Controls basically relate to either quality or cost. For manufactured items, controls may consists of quality assurance checks, in-process feedback systems, or raw material testing. In a staff support role, controls may take the form of authorization approval levels for initiating work or making expenditures, compliance to specified formats for written documents, compliance with specified routines in making purchases (which provides cost-tracking data), and limits on access to certain documents.

Two questions that an employee needs to ask are: (1) Do I fully understand what the controls are (and what they are seeking to control)? and (2) Can I contribute to improving either the effectiveness or efficiency of such controls? Automation is not the panacea that it once was thought to be for improving productivity. Other production factors may play a more significant role in determining throughput rate than the raw speed of the process itself. Systems such as management of supplies, inventory stocking, and management of deliveries can have a significant effect. Automation needs to be considered from the point of view of what overall impact it might have on the operation. For example, in some situations a greater case may be made for automation because of improvements in quality or cost than for productivity alone.

In order to sustain high productivity over a significant period of time, attention must be devoted to keeping the process up and running. This requires effective management of every link in the product delivery chain, namely, suppliers, machinery, company personnel that impact on the process, customer relations, and elements of the external environment. The Japanese have shown us that cultivating good supplier relations and developing efficient systems for doing business with suppliers are extremely important to the profitability of the business. The reliability of machinery used in the process has, of course, a direct effect on productivity. Use of repair data (both from your own records and those of the equipment supplier) can help you anticipate things that are likely to go wrong. Company personnel not directly involved with the process can have just as significant an effect on uptime as direct workers. Maintenance, purchasing, and other central services are continuous process operations in their own right. Close mutual cooperation among these different operations helps assure continuous productivity. Customers themselves affect continuity of the operation. Advance information from customers regarding timing and size of orders is helpful in work-force planning, capacity planning, and scheduling downtimes for maintenance. Accordingly, organizations involved in continuous process operations often spend considerable effort collecting customers' estimates of needs. Finally, there is the external environment that includes players other than just customers and suppliers. Changes in government regulations and actions taken by competitors can affect production options. The actions (or likely actions) of special interest groups can also have an effect.

MEETING DELIVERY DATES

The second performance-evaluation criterion is meeting delivery dates. It is easy for production people to get paranoid about ship dates because of the flak they get from customers and their own management when one is missed. Similarly, the payroll office can never afford to be late in getting checks out. In continuous process operations, delivery dates are expected to be met despite disturbances beyond the control of the responsible organization. The keys to meeting ship dates are *contingency planning* and *work-load balancing*. Contingency planning means having back-up systems in place to handle system breakdowns and overloads. In the case of overloads, good contingency plans have well-established routines for determining job priorities during overload periods. By having such plans and procedures established prior to an actual crisis, the chances are better that they will be accepted as fair and legitimate when they actually have to be employed. Work-load balancing means smoothing out peaks and valleys in work loads. This requires careful scheduling and making judicious tradeoffs to ensure that sufficient resources exist to cover peak demands yet avoid idling personnel and facilities during slack periods. Doing this type of analysis requires skill in system optimization, risk management, and assessment of opportunity costs. Here again, statistics come into play. When data exist on previous operating cycles, such data can be combined with updated information on short-term demand to provide a data base for carrying out regression analyses and making Expected Monetary Value-type calculations. These and other decision support tools can be used to construct near optimum plans for resource management.

MEETING COST OBJECTIVES

The third performance-evaluation measure is meeting cost objectives. A lot can be said about the roles that efficient planning, automation, control, and tracking systems play in meeting cost objectives. Although these are important, they don't have the potential impact of another important element, namely, product design (or redesign). Cost estimates are made based on features that the product must have and the attendant processes that must be used to produce those features. People run into trouble meeting cost objectives when they find out that the processes intended to produce certain features either won't work or are incapable of producing the quality desired. Veterans of continuous process operations know what to do in these situations: Either redesign the product or negotiate less stringent product requirements. This isn't cheating or taking the easy way out. Often, some design specifications are arbitrary and can be loosened without materially affecting product performance. In other cases the product simply may not be embodied in its most elegant form. In these instances design changes may not only improve manufacturing ability but also functionality. In still other cases the marginal benefit to the customer of the original design is not worth the price premium the customer would have to pay to get it. Thus, an important exercise for those involved in continuous process operations to go through is to identify the principal product features that drive costs and contemplate changes (in either features or specifications) that would permit these costs to be reduced. A complicating factor is that "turf" may become an issue. In many instances, individuals charged with implementation are not the same people who have design responsibility. In such cases care must be exercised to avoid alienating the product designer while at the same time conveying the mutual benefits that would derive from the proposed changes.

HANDLING NEW PROJECTS

The fourth element of performance evaluation is handling of new projects. In this instance the continuous process worker acts in the project mode. This component of the job differs little from what a project worker does on a day-to-day basis. The principal difference that does exist is that, for the continuous project worker, the project is not over until the new process has been actually implemented. Thus, the continuous process worker, more so than the project worker, must be concerned with managing the transition from an old system to a new one. How well she or he manages this transition is one component in that person's overall rating for the project.

Managing the transition to a new process requires managing changes in both machinery (either physical hardware or organizational systems) and people. Just as changes in physical hardware are not complete without ensuring that the necessary power and servicing hookups are in place, changes in organizational processes are not complete without linkages that tie them into the operations of the business. The author has seen some new systems meticulously developed, proudly announced, and given only a paper life before being officially retired. The people aspect calls for work-force planning that consists of forecasting needs by skill level and preparing for these new needs through recruitment, retraining, redeployment, and, in some cases, reductions. The important issue here is that project managers give as much attention to "people planning" as they do to planning the reshuffling and retirement of old machinery and systems.

ACHIEVING CUSTOMER SATISFACTION

The final evaluation measure is customer satisfaction. In virtually every case, continuous process workers are involved in producing the final product that is delivered to the customer. They thus can have a considerable impact on those things that traditionally are most important to customers, namely, quality, price, service, courtesy, and product availability. As already mentioned, continuous process workers are often involved in collecting data on who their customers are and what their perceptions are of the firm and its product. This intelligence can form the basis for new product developments that help ensure long-term success of companies. Knowing just what needs fixing is half the battle in providing a more competitive product. Thus, employees engaged in continuous process work should be sure to acquaint themselves with reports on customer feedback. Such information may exist informally if not formally (through letters of correspondence with customers and documentation on meetings). If no significant feedback information exists in any form, then the employee has an opportunity to make an immediate contribution by starting action to obtain such data.

INTERPERSONAL BEHAVIOR: WHERE THE GEARS MESH

How you conduct yourself in your dealings with others will determine whether the organizational wind is at your back or in your face. This section deals with a few basics relating to human relations. Knowledge of these basics will make it easier for you to get your job done.

Drugs and Dress

Interpersonal behavior begins with your control of your own conduct and the image that you present to others. Drugs put people out of control. Drugs change the body chemistry and cause the drug user to respond to others in unnatural ways. Responses tend to be driven by the drug rather than the natural faculties of the user. Regardless of what the user might think, this relinquishing of control decreases effectiveness, produces signs that are easily detected by others, and eventually causes serious errors in judgment. Don't bring drugs (or the influence of drugs) to the workplace. An indication of how seriously employers feel about this issue is the common practice of screening all new employees for drugs during the company medical examination. Blood samples and other tests can reveal the use of drugs for months in the past. In most companies, the detection of harmful drugs means automatic withdrawal of offer of employment. Enough said.

There are very few hard-and-fast rules as to what constitutes proper business attire and good personal appearance. Although a number of books have been written on proper business attire that can guide you in whatever detail you wish, ultimately you must use your own judgment in deciding what is most appropriate for you in your work environment. In most cases it boils down to what looks good. What works for one person might not look good on another. As an example, I will share with you my experience with growing a beard.

It was a time when beards and long hair were fashionable. It was also a time when my hair on top had thinned and my hair line had receded quite a bit. I guess in partial compensation for my loss of hair, I decided to grow a beard. After a couple of months the growth stabilized into what could best be described as a scraggly and loose coalition of hairs. I'm sure the whole episode was quite amusing to some of my colleagues who watched it slowly develop. After some time, when it was apparent that the beard had attained its full growth, one of my subordinates caught me alone in my office. He was a senior employee who had a reputation for being outspoken and calling things just the way he saw them. He started out by saying that he couldn't help but notice that I had been trying to grow a beard. He then offered the disclaimer that whether I wore a beard or not was strictly up to me and he wouldn't offer an opinion as to whether I looked better with or without it. He did, however, want to pass along some advice that his father had once given him. His exact words were, "My father told me that a man should never cultivate on his face, what grows wild on his ass." He then added, "Tom, you just think about that." Then he left. I didn't need anymore hints. The next day the beard was gone.

Some people look good and natural with facial hair while others don't. It is an individual issue that bears little on business as long as it doesn't detract from your appearance or diminish your effectiveness on the job.

How you dress is a visual indication of the level of professionalism that you are bringing to the job. The cleaner, more tasteful, and more appropriate your dress, the more likely it is that others will respond to you in a serious and professional manner. It thus is to your advantage to dress as dapper as the situation will allow without overdoing it. A caveat: You should not dress to the point of either creating a distraction or making yourself look out of place.

All workplaces have either written or implicit dress codes. Observe what these dress codes are for your work situation and make sure that your appearance is on the upper end of the acceptable range.

Listening to Others

You should make a special effort to listen to and understand what others are saying. A common reason for poor listening is that the listener is busy formulating a response while the other person is talking. In doing this one often misses hearing some important information. In other situations an individual may be so anxious to get his or her words in that the speaker is cut off before finishing. When this occurs, the person who is cut off tends to close the ears at the same time that his or her mouth closes. The person may be silent, but instead of listening may only be waiting for another chance to speak. It is better to let a person finish, acknowledge that you heard what was said, and then give your response. In turn, you yourself are more likely to be listened to.

Cooperating with Others

Actively develop a climate of teamwork and cooperation when working with others. Employees are more productive and make things easier for their boss if they are able to get others to willingly support their work efforts. Within a corporation, constant competition exists among groups and individuals for resources to carry out their jobs. Space, money, and facilities are among the things that people compete for. The most valuable resource, however, is a person's time. It takes people to get things done. People will only give you their time if they believe that (1) the activities you are engaged in are worthwhile, and (2) you will reciprocate when they need your help. It is therefore important for you to project a spirit of teamwork and mutual support.

Often the difference between success and failure is the ability to work harmoniously with your peers. This is not always easy, especially when others around you are being tightly squeezed by the pressures of their own work load. Constant pressure builds up irritability in people and leads to short fuses. I can recall one of my own experiences where the defusing of a tense situation helped preserve good relations with one of my peers and simultaneously kept one of my key projects on track.

It was mid-afternoon when one of my best project engineers walked into my office with a serious problem. We were committed to delivering a new product to an important customer in just two months. The product design was complete, but new drawings were needed to incorporate all of the changes that were made to correct problems with the first prototypes. Six weeks were needed to construct new molds to produce the product. This left only two weeks to complete the drafting. Two weeks was enough time, but only if the drafting department could start work right away. That was the rub. The waiting list on new drafting jobs was several weeks long. Every day that our job stayed in the drafting queue meant another day's delay in getting the product to the customer. My engineer was out of options on things to do. He had already talked to the drafting supervisor and had been told that other engineers had jobs waiting to be started that were just as urgent as his. Not only that, his department was understaffed and his people had been working overtime and weekends for some time now to get the backlog down to a reasonable level. They were all dog tired and fed up with trying to do miracles to pull someone else's chestnuts out of the fire. My engineer wanted me to talk to the drafting supervisor to see if I could get our job moved up on the waiting list. I agreed to do what I could.

Walking over to the drafting supervisor's office with my project engineer, I wondered what in the world I could say that would make any difference. The supervisor was a seasoned veteran who had been in his job for many years and had heard it all. Although I was on reasonably good terms with him, I certainly wasn't one of his down-home, poker-playing buddies. I knew that I would get only one shot, for once someone says no, it is difficult to reverse the person's decision.

He wasn't at his desk when we checked by his office. We walked around the corner to the drafting pool and found him talking to some of his people. I recall thinking that this was going to be tough. No type of pressure tactic had any chance of working in this setting. I paused as we stepped just inside the door. The drafting supervisor turned toward us when he saw us walk in. For a moment we stared at each other. Then, in a clear but subdued voice I said, "Bill, I come to you today with my hat in my hand." He cracked up. That was the last thing he expected to hear from me. He broke away from his people and, still smiling, asked what he could do for us. (He already knew what I wanted.) After patiently listening to me explain the urgency of my request, he answered in a non-committal tone, "I'll see what I can do." That was the response I was looking for. It was the closest thing to a yes that I could expect under the circumstances. After we left the drafting room I told my project engineer that we probably would hear from Bill in the next day or so as to when they could start our job. The job was started the next day. There are times when humility can buy you more than any other currency that you have.

Eliminate the buts. It is easy to be critical of other people's ideas. It has been shown, however, that people's neurological response to criticism is the same as their response to a physical blow. It is therefore more conducive to team-building if you can support rather than attack the suggestions of others. Watch yourself. Rather than starting your response with a "Yes, but. . .," it is better to acknowledge the positive aspects of what a person has said and then examine ways to build on the person's ideas to get a better solution. Of course every idea won't work out, but it makes people feel better about their involvement and increases their level of commitment when they see that their ideas are being given fair consideration.

Teamwork demands more than just getting other people to help. You must reciprocate. Reciprocation fuels continued teamwork and also builds your reputation. Being professionals, you can count on your co-workers to acknowledge graciously your contributions to their projects. Thus, your efforts may be showcased in areas outside your immediate organization and increase the number of people that either know you or know of you. This familiarity affects the way others respond to you in future interactions. If nothing else, you tend to be perceived more as "belonging." This subconscious acceptance eliminates one barrier to communication and improves your ability to influence others.

Having pointed out the benefits of helping others, it is important to balance out the picture with a caution: You must not lose sight of your primary responsibility, which is to do the job that you were hired to do. It is great to help others, but make sure that it is not overdone and that your principal responsibilities don't suffer.

Acknowledging the Work of Others

Intellectual honesty is one sign of a competent and confident person. (The converse is also true.) Competent individuals aren't willing to risk tarnishing a hard-earned professional reputation. Confident people feel they can advance through their own achievements.

Not giving proper credit can kill you in several ways. First, the person who was slighted won't be overly enthusiastic about helping you in the future. In fact, that individual will probably go on a personal crusade to spread the news of your theft to your colleagues, who might, in turn, become reluctant to work with you on future projects. Second, your own management might start to question your honesty and whether they can rely on what you tell them. Others might begin questioning how much of your previous work was actually done by someone else. People who use your work and identify you as the originator might be embarrassed at some other time when they are corrected as to who originally did the work.

There are just too many ways to lose. To be safe, err on the side of giving too much credit as opposed to too little. Check your acknowledgments and distribution list on written material. Check your list of references to ensure that you cite appropriate published works and any unpublished work or private correspondence that you make use of. Invite significant contributors to co-author papers with you. (This applies even if the person is your boss.) On oral presentations, mention at the beginning those who worked with you.

The message contained in the saying "Praise in public and criticize in private" is that praise is most appreciated when done openly and criticism is less resented when done on a one-on-one basis. It therefore benefits all parties concerned when you thoughtfully and generously acknowledge the contributions of others.

Using Charm: Catching More Flies with Honey

You can be nice with the same amount of effort that it takes to be rude. The difference is that if you are nice you are more likely to get the help you need from others inside the company. After all, the workplace has seen plenty of S.O.B.'s and it is refreshing to meet someone different.

Charm means using tact, warmth, and wit to influence others. As a good example of tact, when going over typographical errors with a typist, it is better to say, "I have a change to make" as opposed to "You made a mistake." In the first statement no fault is assigned, hence no one's feelings should be hurt. Besides, it is irrelevant who is to blame; what you are really interested in is getting the document straightened out. To cap it all off, harried typists get people coming in all day telling them about the mistakes that they have made. They don't need any more putdowns from you.

Make a habit of smiling. Aside from the fact that people respond more positively to a smile than a frown, it will make you feel better. In addition, research has shown that people ascribe more intelligence to people who smile. Thus, in both a literal and figurative sense, a smile can make you look brighter. Because half of your waking time will be spent on the job, it makes sense to relax and get as much satisfaction out of your work as circumstances will permit. Maintaining a positive frame of mind will help you get more pleasure from your job and make the workplace more pleasant for those who interact with you.

Avoiding Personal Conflict

Technical disagreements are one thing, but personality clashes are deadly. Technical disagreements involve issues that can be resolved through sufficient analysis, experimentation, or research. Personality conflicts are just that. You may clash with someone because of the person's attitude, the way you think he or she feels about you, your lack of respect for the person, or any number of other reasons. Whatever the cause and regardless of who is right, personal conflicts hurt both parties.

There is a saying, "A person who stops to throw a rock at every dog that barks never gets anywhere." That's a colorful way of saying that you don't have to respond to every cheap shot and you don't always have to have the last word. If you do you will waste so much time and energy in petty conflicts that you won't be able to make progress on what really counts.

When personal conflicts do surface, there are always two sides to the story. Allegations are made by both parties. It is a messy business. Even if you are eventually vindicated, the seed has been planted, and management may harbor some lingering suspicions about your ability to get along with others. The net result is that at best you end up with one strike against you. Should another flap arise between you and another individual, management will start to take a very hard look at you. It thus is clear that personal conflicts produce no winners.

A long-lasting residue from personality clashes is the enemies they produce. Unfortunately, enemies in the work-place don't go away. They last for years and even decades. Their presence detracts from the pleasantness of your work situation and can limit your range of influence. The best way to deal with enemies is not to make any to begin with.

One technique that is useful in defusing tense situations is to refer to people by their first name when talking to them. For example, instead of saying "I believe that the way to handle this is to. . . ," it is better to say, "Sandy, I believe that the way to handle this is to. . . ." Not much difference in wording, but it makes a big difference in the tone of the conversation. The insertion of a person's first name sends the message that you are still dealing with that individual as a person and not as a nameless adversary. It has a calming effect and makes it easier for the other party to concentrate on the real issue at hand as opposed to personal jostling.

Cultivating a Positive, Alert Image

In day-to-day interactions there are many little things that you can do that will sharpen your image. When you answer the phone you should state your name and possibly company name with authority. For example: "Janet Becker," or "Extension 3919, Janet Becker," or "ABC company, Janet Becker," whatever suits your style. A simple "Hello" is unacceptable.

When making a phone call it is standard practice to first announce your name, company name, and then ask for the person with whom you wish to speak. If you don't volunteer that information you will have to give it anyway before you can proceed with a business conversation. Be sharp; don't make people ask you for something that you should have already given them.

As often as not you won't reach your party on the first call. In those instances it is important that you don't let the person answering the phone off the hook. It is poor practice to just leave your phone number (or worse yet to simply say you will call back later). Leave a message. Let the person know what you are calling about and what it is you need. In some instances the person answering will be able to help you directly. In other cases if the party returns your call and catches you away from your desk, the caller may be able to leave the information that you need with the person (or machine) who answers your phone. You thus may get what you are after without ever speaking with the person directly, just by leaving an intelligent message. There is yet one other benefit of identifying the purpose of your call; a person is more likely to return your call promptly when that individual has been alerted to what it is about.

Another way to look sharp is to remember names. We have all had experiences where we have just been introduced to a person but we can't for the life of us remember the person's name. A technique for remembering names is to first listen, repeat it when greeting the person ("Nice to meet you, *Bob*"), and then form a mental association of the person with the name. For example, you may recall other people you know with the same first name and visualize them among those people. Or you may associate the person's name with one of the person's prominent physical features. For example, "bald Bob" or "tall Tom" or the like. One warning: When making such associations, be sure to avoid making Freudian slips.

In face-to-face interactions you can project a sharp image by speaking distinctly and coherently. Be direct and concise. When answering questions, take care to provide complete information, but don't ramble; that is, don't digress too far from the subject, and when you have finished, stop talking.

Practice looking others in the eye (or the bridge of the nose if you are shy). My curiosity has helped me overcome my own shyness in looking others directly in the eye. Studies on human responses have found that the pupil of the eye dilates when it sees something that it likes and contracts when it sees something it dislikes. The change in size is the key factor and not the absolute size of the pupil. I am always curious to see how people really feel toward me and I check this out at the start of most conversations. I also check back from time to time to see how they are responding to things that I am saying.

When others are speaking, you can show that you are alert and understand what they are saying by paraphrasing their important points and playing them back to them. This is an active listening technique that is safe and easy to use. Not only does this signal to the speaker that you are listening, but it also affords the speaker the opportunity to correct you on anything that you have misheard. Using active listening techniques like this one helps safeguard against the other person walking away thinking that you didn't understand a word that was said. Instead, they are more likely to go away thinking that you are a pretty sharp person.

Demonstrating Maturity: What Constitutes Maturity and How to Show It

Signs of maturity include (1) treating issues seriously, (2) not becoming embroiled in petty issues, and (3) accepting responsibility for your actions.

TREATING ISSUES SERIOUSLY

Treating issues seriously means assuming that issues at hand are real and that you will have to live with whatever decisions you make. It also means approaching matters with a proactive attitude and not resting until either your responsibilities have been fulfilled or the issue has been resolved. A serious approach to problem solving starts with a determination of the options available for attacking the problem. The next step is to scrutinize these options and select the best one, considering factors such as degrees of risk, expected return on investment, time constraints, financial considerations, safety, and probability of success. After making a selection, you should get some action started right away. Don't rest until the ball is out of your court and you know when you can expect it to return.

A proactive attitude does not mean rushing headlong into every perceived problem. A trait of maturity is the practice of rationally sizing up situations before launching out on solutions. Not all problems *are* real, and you can burn up a lot of time and energy chasing phantoms. A way of getting started that guards against chasing false problems is to try to quantify the problem. (In fact, a measure of how well you understand the problem is the degree to which you can quantify it.) Possible ways of quantifying the severity of a problem are by monitoring its frequency of occurrence, measuring its intensity, and assessing its economic impact. This quantification process not only can answer the question of whether the problem warrants any further investigation, but it can also give you some insight as to just what it is that you ought to be attacking. It can also provide a gauge for monitoring progress in eliminating the problem.

AVOIDING PETTY ISSUES

Another aspect of maturity is not allowing yourself to become bogged down in petty issues. The key to avoiding this pitfall lies in maintaining a proper perspective. In some cases individuals get entangled in a controversy that degenerates to the point where winning the argument is more important than moving forward on the work. In other cases an employee may raise some arcane procedural point of order that serves more to establish turf than to correct a legitimate problem. In all cases, petty issues are ones that can be easily resolved provided that the parties involved are willing to put aside prejudices and act rationally. If you find that another individual is allowing prejudices to interfere with his or her rationality, rather than tell the person off, you might try, "I don't understand why you say that," or "The information that I have doesn't agree with what you say." If you find yourself in a situation where a lot of controversy is raging over a trivial matter (other than face-saving) try to terminate the conflict with, "What do you propose?" Often you will find that the actions suggested by the opposing party are not that much different from what you would suggest. Listen to the other party's suggestions and try to be accommodating.

Finally, some general advice on how you should conduct yourself in a conflict situation is to: (1) *Stay calm.* Try to maintain your professionalism and objectivity. You can help maintain your objectivity by remembering that the most important thing is not how you got into this mess but how you are going to get out of it. If you should find yourself involved in a meeting that has degenerated into a fault-finding session, you can help get things back on track and demonstrate maturity at the same time by saying something to the effect, "I understand the concern for how we got into this position, but the issue that we need to address is where do we go from here." Or, "Our time would be better spent on formulating a plan for recovery." (2) *Don't ascribe unsubstantiated motives to the other party.* Psychologists have demonstrated time and again that all of us are awfully poor judges of what is going on in another person's mind. (3) *Be truthful.* Misrepresentations and exaggerations eventually work to your detriment. (4) *Don't be vindictive.* Don't go out of your way to nail the other person or to get even.

ACCEPTING RESPONSIBILITY FOR YOUR ACTIONS

The third aspect of maturity, accepting responsibility for your actions, means shouldering your share of the blame when things go wrong. This is a hard thing to do. We commonly see people in responsible positions try to absolve themselves of blame in the wake of disaster. A typical statement might be: "I accept total responsibility for what happened. . .but the situation was beyond anyone's control." This type of response never did anyone much good. People who use it end up looking like weasels. People respond in this way because they are afraid of punitive actions. This is a valid concern. You will not, however, make yourself look any better by ducking responsibility. Better techniques exist for ameliorating the situation and minimizing negative consequences to you. The most immediate things you can do are: (1) assure those affected that this failure was not due to a lack of concern about your responsibilities, (2) put this failure in perspective by citing your previous record of success, and (3) assure others that you are committed to not letting a similar failure occur in the future. The next thing is to launch a strong recovery effort as soon as possible. The recovery effort should have an investigative phase to identify just what went wrong and an aggressive rebuilding phase to get back on track quickly. Doing an outstanding job during the recovery phase can nearly offset the negative marks you may have received earlier on. One thing to keep in mind: What works in your favor is that your performance rating will probably span a period over which you handled several assignments. One mistake will generally not be enough to wreck your entire rating. A winning strategy, therefore, is to excel on whatever other projects that you have going and thereby fuel the perception that your one subpar performance was just an isolated event. A word of caution, however: Operate within your limits. Give solidly professional efforts, but don't press beyond your ability.

The traits that demonstrate maturity do not accrue to a person simply by growing older. With age you generally recognize the importance of these traits and work on them accordingly. The message is that they are just as important now as they will be five years from now. You should work now to make them a consistent part of your makeup.

Cultivating Good Relations with Co-workers

In this section a great deal will be said regarding your relations with co-workers. As a point of clarification, the term *co-workers* is meant to refer to the full range of employees that you might interact with, not just cohorts; that is, employees who joined the company the same year as you did.

Co-workers are an integral part of the work environment, and they can have a strong influence on the success of a new employee. They constitute an informal but powerful force. There are many ways that they can help you and just as many ways for them to make things more difficult for you. You need to be familiar with techniques for getting the most out of your interactions with co-workers.

CO-WORKERS AS IMPORTANT SOURCES
OF INFORMATION

One of the problems that new employees face is that they don't know what it is that they don't know. In trying to get information from a fellow worker you might find yourself in a position of having to ask just the right question before the other party will give you any useful information. A humorous story illustrates this scenario.

During tryouts in a youth basketball league, the coach noticed that one of the kids was significantly smaller than the others. Observing this child closely, he also saw that the child was not as coordinated as most of the other players. This raised the coach's suspicion, for the minimum age requirement was seven and in previous years some parents had tried to enter their children in the program who were younger than seven. Because young children are not as sophisticated in telling falsehoods as their more experienced parents, the coach thought he might be able to ferret out the truth from the child if he used a somewhat oblique approach. He went over to the child, put his hand on his shoulder, kneeled down on one knee, and asked him his name. The child answered, "Brian." "Well, Brian," asked the coach, "what date is your birthday?" Brian quickly responded with, "October 15th." Not getting quite the information he was looking for, the coach asked, "What year?" Brian then looked the coach straight in the eye and after a pause replied, "Every year."

It is obviously better for someone to volunteer information than for you to have to pry it out of them. (Even after you've finished prying you can never be sure you have all the available information that you need.) A good approach to generating open dialogue is to begin by telling the other people just what you are trying to do. Let them know what information you already have and what information you believe you need. Then ask if they can tell you where you might be able to get the needed information and if there is anything you have overlooked. Because the other person knows your ultimate objective, he or she is in a position to make a judgment as to whether you are headed in the right direction and whether the information you are seeking will help you get there. If people can't help you directly, they probably will be able to steer you to someone who can.

In addition to guiding you through organizational routines and supplying background information on projects, co-workers can provide information that you would never think to ask about. For example, they might tip you off about pet dislikes your boss might have—what triggers his or her rage button (or they might decide it would be more fun to watch you find out for yourself). The list of possible pet peeves is endless: documenting poorly, showing up unprepared, not following instructions, not following prescribed company procedures, coming in late, leaving early, smoking, chewing gum, biting your nails, chewing tobacco, and on and on. You can't worry yourself about what pet peeves your boss may possibly have. If you do you will go nuts. Your co-workers, however, already know the nature of the beast. If they think you are worth the time, they might tell you how to stay on the tame side.

CO-WORKERS AS COACHES

If they are anything, veteran co-workers are survivors. They have been through the wars and along the way developed survival routines that have pulled them through. As various situations arise, you can benefit by having them share with you some of their approaches for handling difficult situations.

One of the most effective routines that I learned about dealing with bosses came from a crafty co-worker named John Baden. I once had a hard-driving boss who pushed his people just as hard as he pushed himself. He was constantly piling on additional assignments—each one important and having an urgent completion date. For the most part these small emergencies were not extraordinarily difficult, and they could be handled with a week or less of full-time attention. The problem was that these emergencies and quickie jobs came in more rapidly than they could be disposed of, thereby disrupting work on prior emergencies and completely playing havoc with completion of long-range projects. I usually wasn't very successful in arguing against the merits of the new work. And even when I was, my boss would remain unsatisfied and would be visibly annoyed. I was equally unsuccessful in getting additional help for my work. In so many words, my boss would argue, "Surely this one little additional straw won't break your back."

John Baden suggested to me a winning approach. John said that rather than fight with my boss on reducing the work load to a manageable level, let my boss make the decision himself as to which projects deserved the most urgent attention. This was good advice and I proceeded to lay the groundwork to take advantage of it. First, I compiled a complete list of my work projects, their current status, scheduled milestones, and completion dates. I then noted what percentage of my time was being spent on each project. I was now ready for the next mini-emergency that might come along.

I didn't have to wait long. The next day my boss called me into his office with a new crisis. After carefully listening to him describe the problem and making sure that I clearly understood how much effort would be required to handle it, I gave my response. I started with, "I recognize that this is a serious problem and I agree that something has to be done about it. But what I need help on is establishing priorities. As you know, we have pressing completion dates on a number of other projects." At this point I pulled out my schedule and quickly reviewed the current jobs and their planned completion dates. I concluded with the key question, "Currently these existing projects are consuming all of my people's time. Which of these projects do you want me to drop or postpone?" My boss was now in the position of having to make the hard decision himself. He could have tossed the decision back in my lap, but he didn't. What he did do was suggest that we postpone doing anything on the new problem for a while. By responding as I did, I had just become a better employee and at the same time done a service for my boss. Because I concisely reviewed my work projects, he was better able to put them in perspective and arrive at rational priorities. (He was also reminded of the heavy work load that my people were carrying.) We both won.

I judiciously used this same routine at other times when it seemed like I was being presented with conflicting demands. As a consequence, I began getting more support for my work and, in time, had less and less need to resort to this technique.

Not all of your co-workers' advice will be good. You will have to judge for yourself which of it to use. The best advice usually stems from common sense but, nevertheless, may be something that would take you some time to discover by yourself. Co-workers can tell you what has worked for them and can help you develop your own inventory of successful routines.

CO-WORKERS AS INFLUENTIAL PEOPLE

Veteran co-workers are known quantities and have already established their credibility. It doesn't matter whether a particular veteran employee habitually exaggerates, understates, or calls it straight, management already has that person calibrated and can draw some conclusions from what he or she says. For example, in a casual conversation with your boss, a co-worker might say, "The company sure made a good decision when it decided to hire Susan. She's really a dedicated worker." Nobody asked for this opinion, but there it is and the statement can't be erased. It plants a seed and gets people thinking in a particular direction.

In more formal situations a co-worker can be one of your first advocates. It is not unusual for management to discuss staffing of projects with workers before final assignments are handed out. (It is rare that employees are given complete latitude on selecting which projects they work on, but often employees are asked how they might feel about working on a particular project.) Managers tend to pride themselves on their independent thinking; nevertheless, they can be influenced by people closer to the situation than they are. Co-workers who think highly of your ability can be helpful in getting you opportunities that you deserve.

CO-WORKERS AS FRIENDS

It is to your advantage to have a wide circle of acquaintances. (This is called *plugging into the network.*) You will find it easier to approach others for help when they already know you. Further, they will be more willing to spend a significant amount of time with you and make a serious attempt to be helpful when you are a familiar face.

An easy and natural way to meet people is at the lunch table. You will find that most of your co-workers eat lunch at a specific time everyday. By varying the time of day that you go to lunch, you can broaden the range of people that you meet. We are all such creatures of habit that not only do we get into a routine of eating at a specific time, but also in a specific section of the dining room. Over a period of time, informal boundaries develop that separate territorial eating spaces for various departments within the organization. Don't be intimidated; there's nothing sacred about these territorial boundaries. Join in, sit down, and introduce yourself.

Aside from being a good place to meet people, the lunch table is a forum for exchange of information. Both company business and items of general interest are discussed. The latest developments on hot projects, new business opportunities, pending organizational changes, what's going on in the industry, and important upcoming events are typical business topics. Nonbusiness discussions can be equally helpful, especially when they deal with recreational or financial matters. You can find out about interesting things that are going on in the community and get some ideas about how you might want to manage your financial affairs.

Summarizing, the lunch table not only helps your exposure (what you see), visibility (who sees you), and networking (getting plugged in), but it also helps keep you in touch with significant things going on inside and outside the company.

DEALING WITH YOUR BOSS: MUTUAL DEPENDENCE

Throughout this section, the "boss" is often referred to in the masculine gender. This is not done with any sexist intent, but rather is done solely to facilitate clarity in reading. Whenever crispness and clarity of thought are not sacrificed, a neutral gender is used.

The relationship between you and your boss should be harmonious and mutually supporting. Your boss should play many roles: mentor, coach, teacher, advocate, role model, and, of course, captain of the ship. Though you may be highly dependent on him, the relationship between you and your boss should be one between two mature adults, not a parent-child relationship.

The relationship should not be an adversarial one as is classically depicted in the comic strip involving Dagwood Bumstead and his boss, Mr. Dithers. This stereotype of the boss depicts him as the villain who stands between us and all the rewards that we want and deserve. He is an obstacle to be overcome. He is also the person who robs us of our freedom by commanding us to do his bidding as opposed to letting us exercise our initiative to do what really needs to be done. Such views are not only distorted but they also put people who buy into them at a tremendous disadvantage. Individuals with such attitudes tend to behave in ways that stimulate conflict and polarize relationships. Both parties suffer. A healthier and more accurate view of the relationship is one between two team members. Your boss wins when you win and vice versa. You may not agree on every issue, but success is most often achieved when you can minimize your differences and pull together.

Get Your Priorities Straight

Bear in mind that during your first six months on the job, you are not trying to work your boss for a promotion. You are just trying not to get fired. Your primary objectives are creating a good impression, establishing a good working relationship, and providing him with the support that he needs from you. This section discusses what actions you can take that will better assure that these three things happen.

Hear Your Boss

Often when a boss is critiquing an employee's performance or merely offering work-related advice, an employee may become so defensive that he or she fails to get the message that the boss is trying to get across. The boss may or may not be trying to assign fault, but even so, it is probably secondary to achieving some other result. Independent of what has happened until now, your boss wants to pursue a particular course of action. It is up to you to (1) keep your ears open long enough to hear what it is and (2) act promptly to give your boss what he wants.

To show your boss that he has been heard and to assure yourself that you have an accurate understanding of your marching orders, it is good practice to use the same technique with your boss as you do with others: Summarize in your own words what you believe the boss's instructions or suggestions are. When you play this back to him you will be surprised to see how his face lights up with satisfaction. But don't let it end at that. If it is a new assignment, make sure you know what the expected completion date is. If it requires getting information or some other input from others, ask for suggestions as to who are the appropriate contacts. Finally, if it is a lengthy assignment, you may want to get on your boss's calendar now for your first status review.

Work to Establish a Good Relationship

A favorite quote of mine deals with the boss-subordinate relationship: *In industry, nobody loves you but your supervisor.*

This is a lighthearted way of making the point that if your supervisor doesn't support you, no one else will. It therefore is essential that your relationship with your boss be a good one.

To have a good relationship requires mutual respect and much more. It also requires working toward a consistent set of goals (goal congruence), satisfying mutual expectations, and having compatible work styles. The primary responsibility is up to you—the subordinate—to establish a good working relationship with your boss. To do this you need to determine your boss's long-term objective for your work, his definition of success, and the manner of conducting business that best suits his psychological makeup. You also need to let the boss know how you view your job and what you expect to get out of it.

It is helpful to have your work put in perspective. Ask your boss for ideas on how your job assignment contributes toward satisfying the overall objectives of the organization. Also ask for what is envisioned as an ideal outcome of your work (definition of success). Be careful here. Make sure that your boss understands that you are not asking how to do the job or what the solution is to your problem, but rather what would be an ideal end result. These two inputs will help keep you headed in the right direction and guard against you either overworking the problem or stopping short of an acceptable solution.

One of the things necessary for a good working relationship is to have compatible (if not matching) styles. Try to be synchronized with the style of your manager. For example, some bosses like to know full details and be given frequent status reports of what is happening on a project. Others prefer to have a general understanding of what is going on and be advised only when trouble spots develop or changes are being contemplated in project schedules. A boss who prefers the latter style might be annoyed if you are continually turning in status reports.

As another example, some managers emphasize a methodical work approach. For them, it is of prime importance to have well-laid-out schedules and to adhere closely to prescribed routines for doing business. For such managers it is important that you demonstrate that you are in control of things. For managers who prize productivity, it may be more important to get into action quickly, maintain a fast pace, and come up with quick results. Both styles have their merits. However, the key point for you to remember is that in order for your work to be best appreciated, your style needs to mesh with that of your boss.

Properly Prepare for Meetings with Your Boss

Gather and organize relevant information before meeting with your boss (or others, for that matter, but especially with your boss) and present it in a professional manner appropriate to the situation. If a problem exists on your project and some action needs to be taken, be prepared to answer such questions as, "What are you doing to correct the situation?" and "What do you propose that we do?"

Keep Your Boss Informed

No boss likes to be caught by surprise. Specifically, there are two situations that often arise where it is critical that your supervisor be kept informed. One is when something occurs that threatens a project schedule. For example, a supplier may be behind in deliveries or some work task may be taking longer than planned. Any number of unexpected setbacks may arise. Keep in mind that when serious problems do develop, they won't get any better by covering them up. Inform your boss while there is still some time to do something about them! (Or at least before the situation deteriorates any further.)

The other situation deals with bad news. If there is bad news concerning your project, you should be the one to inform your boss about it. Don't let your supervisor be put in an awkward situation by getting hit with bad news from a peer (or worse yet, his or her boss) about something that falls within your supervisor's own area of responsibility. The last thing that your boss wants others to think is that he or she doesn't know what is going on within his or her own shop. Furthermore, if you allow your boss to be taken by surprise, he has no opportunity to assess the seriousness of the situation and formulate a well-thought-out response. You have put your boss out of control.

Many situations arise where your boss needs timely and accurate information from you, but the two situations cited above are the ones where lack of such information can do you and your boss the most harm.

Make Your Boss Look Good

The primary responsibility of any employee is to make one's boss look good. The better you make the boss look, the more likely this person is to feel good about your work and the more support you will receive. Moreover, the stronger standing your boss has within the organization, the more he is able to protect the welfare of his subordinates.

You make your boss look good not by overinflating his image or doing his work for him, but by complementing his strengths and taking care of your responsibilities in a way that reflects favorably on him. Things like meeting your project completion dates, keeping the boss informed on critical issues, and making sure that he has up-to-date information before going into important meetings are all ways of making the boss look good.

Show that you are working as a team and singing off the same sheet of music. Avoid disagreements in front of others. Ask yourself, "Is this an issue that must be settled now or can we work it out after the meeting?" On the other hand, do not hesitate to come to your boss's aid quickly if he or she makes an error that is serious enough that it must be corrected immediately or if your boss is floundering while answering a question. Sometimes you can do this gracefully by leading with a qualifier. For example, in response to your boss making an incorrect statement, you might say, "Bill, I know that that is what I told you a while back, but since then we have new information that says. . . ." When your boss is groping for assistance in answering a question, you might say something like, "The current answer to that question is. . ." or "This number is subject to change, but. . ." or something that would fit the situation. What you are trying to do is save face for your boss by implying that there is some valid reason for him not knowing information someone might reasonably expect him to know. In other words, use skill to avoid unnecessary embarrassment for your boss. You would do it for a friend. Your boss will do it for you.

Think about your boss's strong points (okay, think harder). Praise those points when others ask about your boss and lean on them to help you get your job done. For example, if your boss has a forceful image, take advantage of this when seeking cooperation from others by letting them know that your boss is behind the particular idea. Conversely, help your boss with his weak points by providing whatever support you can.

Don't Criticize Your Boss to Others

Criticizing your boss hurts you in several ways. First, as a new employee you can't possibly be aware of all the pipelines that exist for feeding information back to your boss. What you say in private and in confidence may, nevertheless, find its way back to your boss and create problems in your relationship with your boss.

A second way it can hurt you is to tarnish your image. Potshots can make you look devious and earn you a reputation as a griper and a nonteam player. Others may very well think to themselves, "If this is what he says about his own boss, what might he say about me when my back is turned?" They might also ask, "If your complaints are valid, why don't you take them directly to your boss?" This calls into question your honesty, courage, and ability to communicate with superiors.

As a team player you are expected to go along with the program once it has been finalized, even though you may disagree with the approach or the objective itself. (Of course, this does not apply when issues such as morality, legality, or ethics are in question.) When you don't act like a team player, you make others have second thoughts about working on projects with you.

No one, including your boss, is going to be right 100 percent of the time. If you loudly advertise your disagreement with your boss, and the boss turns out to be right, you can end up looking both disloyal and not-too-bright. Even in those situations where you turn out to be right, you won't gain much since everyone knows that it is easy to second-guess when you don't have to carry the burden of the decision.

Criticizing your boss can hurt you in a way that you may have a hard time recognizing. The process of articulating your boss's faults can coalesce and intensify any negative feelings that you have toward your boss. Such feelings are likely to be projected in your interactions with your boss. (Either that, or you will have to work especially hard to conceal these feelings.) Related to this is the fact that people find it difficult to change their mind on a subject once they have openly stated their position. Accordingly, it will be harder for you internally to come to peace with your boss once you have voiced your criticism, whether your boss hears about it or not.

Even though we all have occasions where we want to blow off steam, the subject of your boss is off-limits. Keep your thoughts to yourself and don't allow yourself to be prodded into making dumb remarks. Usually your boss's shortcomings are well known to others and they don't have to be advertised by you.

Accept Criticism in a Positive Fashion

No one likes to be criticized. It takes some effort to accept criticism positively, but the ability to do so can work in your favor.

The important thing to remember is that you should concern yourself more with hearing what the criticism is than erecting a defense (or finding an excuse). That is not to say that you shouldn't defend yourself if the criticism is not justified or there are extenuating circumstances. It is, however, your first obligation to acknowledge that you heard the criticism and that you understand what your boss wants. You may then tell your side of the story. Finish on a positive note by reiterating that you understand the reason for the criticism and that you will give this area your attention.

Make Effective Use of Performance Reviews

Performance reviews are trying on both boss and subordinate. At their best, they are one more administrative headache for the boss. At their worst, they expose chasms of differences of opinion and place a psychological strain on the boss-subordinate relationship. For these reasons performance reviews tend to be rather antiseptic. They often are long on praise of good traits and short on shortcomings. For example, consider the performance write-up that says, "John is bright, conscientious, and works well with others. His written communication skills should improve with practice." These sentences say nothing about his work accomplishments and disguise the fact that John doesn't write well and doesn't do it very often.

TIPS ON GETTING USABLE FEEDBACK

For your own good you may have to draw out criticism from your boss. If you don't find out what is really bothering him, then you won't be able to address your perceived weaknesses. Your boss may feel that you have significant shortcomings (and may even discuss them with others in management), but may not state them to you directly for fear of a confrontation. You need to make the situation less threatening. A good way to do this is to ask the question, "If you *had* to identify an area that I was weakest in, what would it be?" This gets your boss off the hook. Now having asked the question, it is up to you to sit back and take it. If you react defensively or emotionally, you will never get a straight answer out of that person again.

Try to keep in mind that your primary purpose is to collect information that will help you turn in a better performance in the upcoming year. In some companies your raise is not determined until after the performance review meeting between you and your boss and, consequently, helping your manager come to an accurate assessment of your performance is an important objective of the meeting. In other companies your raise is determined prior to your meeting with your boss. In all cases, however, the performance review is an opportunity to collect feedback on performance that can make you a more valuable employee in the future.

During the meeting you should take notes so that you can be sure to follow up on any action items that develop. Such items include any job responsibilities that you have not yet completed, objectives for the upcoming year, and agreements that commit either of you to specific actions. Don't conclude the meeting before mapping out a plan to address specific weaknesses. A good plan should include clearly identifiable milestones and scheduled feedback on progress.

HOW TO PROVIDE YOUR OWN INPUT

As already indicated, some companies invite employees to provide input to their own performance evaluation. Employees may be asked to write up their accomplishments during the past year and to get together with management to formulate plans for improving their work skills. Seize this opportunity. Don't be bashful about talking about all the good things you have done. My grandmother always told me, "It's a poor dog that won't wag his own tail." This is your chance to make sure that your boss and others have the proper perspective on your contributions during the year. You can be more effective in creating that perspective by following the suggestions given below.

Put some effort into your write-up. Don't just assume your supervisor knows how you spent your time. Even though he or she does know, others who may read your write-up may not. Write it in such a way that anyone could read it and adequately understand what your contributions were over the past year. The quality of your work is one thing, but how well you describe it is another. Be aware that others who read your write-up may view it as an indicator of your writing skills.

Indicate your major contributions and how they benefited the company. You short-change yourself when you only list the projects that you worked on and the tasks that you performed. You also need to provide the reader with an interpretation of what impact your work has had, or is likely to have, on the business. For example, you might include a phrase like, ". . . these innovations were responsible for increasing the product yield from 15 percent to 75 percent."

It is also a good idea to provide an estimate of what percentage of your time you spent on each of the major items that you discuss. The amount of space that you devote to discussing any item should be in proportion to its importance (or in proportion to the time that you spent on them if two or more items have roughly the same significance). If you devote too much space to discussing small projects that took up, say, less than 5 percent of your time, then you will lose focus and others will lose track of the one or two really important items. (Flooding the document with relatively unimportant contributions will also give the impression that you are just trying to add filler to an unproductive year.)

Discuss your most important contributions first and then move on to other projects in decreasing order of importance.

State what you did personally. If you were part of a team effort, state what your contribution was, not just the charter of the team. Also be careful not to give the impression that you are taking credit for someone else's work.

Place the main emphasis on your mainstream respon-sibilities. Although you certainly don't want to overlook your peripheral contributions (services performed for the company that fall outside the charter of your primary work assignment), don't devote an inordinate amount of space to them. For example, you might only wish to say, "Departmental Coordinator for the United Way fund-raising campaign" or "Member of the Safety Committee." These jobs are well known to your organization and you need not describe your duties in detail. Unless you made some unusual contribution, be as brief as possible.

Get it in on time. Most employees hate doing performance write-ups, and bosses hate having to pull the darn things out of them. Don't be another headache for your boss. Hand it in when it is asked for.

It is actually to your advantage to get your write-up in about a week before it is due. This will be ahead of most of your colleagues and will allow your boss to give it some individualized attention. Ask your boss to look it over and get suggested changes back to you in time for you to submit a revised copy.

Be Traceable

On occasions, your boss will need to get in touch with you immediately: to give you an urgent assignment, obtain information that only you may have, or seek your advice on a decision that must be made in real time. In those situations it is disruptive to the business and disappointing to your boss when you cannot be found. The longer your whereabouts remain unknown, the dimmer view a boss or supervisor takes of the episode, even when it turns out that you were on legitimate business.

In some situations your disappearance can make both you and your boss look bad. For example, your boss may need you to sit in on an impromptu meeting or, worse yet, your boss's superior may be looking for you. When your boss can't turn you up, it advertises your elusiveness and makes your boss look out of control.

You can make yourself look like a polished professional by being traceable. Let your boss or the boss's secretary know if you will be away from your desk for a significant length of time. Indicate where you can be reached and what time you expect to be back. If for some reason you don't want to bother your boss or the secretary, then leave a note in a conspicuous place on your desk. This scores points for you by demonstrating maturity and responsibility. It also tacitly makes the point that you feel that your work is of such importance that someone may need to urgently meet with you at any time.

In addition to being traceable today, your boss and others should be able to determine your availability in upcoming days. Such information is needed for scheduling meetings and making work plans. It therefore is a good practice to make a note of business meetings, planned vacation, and appointments on your calendar and leave your calendar open on your desk (or have it accessible through your computer terminal). This allows others to know what your schedule is even when you are not around. (It is acceptable to take your calendar with you to meetings in which you may need it.) This is especially helpful to people trying to schedule meetings involving a number of individuals. Your boss will see this practice as a sign of professionalism, and the secretaries will love you.

Follow Up on Assignments

Recognize when you have been given an assignment. A typical failing of new employees is not following up on action items given by their boss. For example, a boss may casually mention that a subordinate might want to search out the facts on some particular matter (or give someone a call, or check into the feasibility of some idea). What the employee may have interpreted as only a suggestion may have, in fact, been meant as a direct order. Later, when the boss finds out that the subordinate has not followed up on the request, the boss may feel that the employee isn't taking his or her work seriously enough and is ignoring managerial guidance. None of this is good for the subordinate.

A way to protect against these types of miscommunications is to jot down immediately all suggestions and direct orders from your boss. Just doing this has an immediate positive effect on bosses. They can clearly see that you are listening to them and are preparing to take some action. If you don't have a notebook handy, use whatever is available. If you can't write a note right away, you should make it a point to record the action item just as soon as possible. After you have gotten it down, post it with your list of other action items and start something going on it right away. Continue to follow up on it until you have something definitive to report to your boss.

CHAPTER SIX

STANDARDS
OF PROFESSIONAL
PERFORMANCE

A good performer is someone who focuses his or her energy on the right issues and handles those issues well. This chapter summarizes what these issues are and provides scales by which performance levels can be measured. The intent of this chapter is to provide enough information to allow new employees to answer for themselves the question: "How am I doing?"

PRINCIPAL DETERMINANTS: WHAT ENTERS INTO THE EVALUATION EQUATION

Although there are many different items that can figure into the evaluation of your overall performance—and this list varies from job to job and from company to company—there are several universal ones that collectively carry, say, 80 percent of the weight. Seven of the most important ones are discussed below in their approximate order of importance.

One thing that should be kept in mind is that it is not necessary to be a jack-of-all-trades. You don't have to shine in all areas. Doing one thing extremely well may be sufficient if it corresponds to the thing that your boss thinks is most important and if it matches the needs of the job.

Ethics: Preserving Professional Trust

This item is sometimes overlooked because it is not something for which you get positive strokes. It is taken for granted. It is nothing to brag about if you have it, but it can destroy you if you don't. The following sections examine various abuses of professional trust.

PROTECTING COMPANY ASSETS:
PURCHASES, VOUCHERS, PROPERTY,
AND TIME

As a professional, you are put in a position where you must manage company assets. Such assets include money, material, proprietary information, and time. If you use such assets for personal gain or fail to guard against their misuse, then you are violating the trust placed in you as a professional.

Don't steal from the company! This is one thing that can end your career more abruptly than anything else. Once you have shown yourself to be a thief, there is virtually nothing anyone can do to intercede on your behalf. All the good things that you might have done up to that point are of no consequence. You can't be trusted. You are finished.

There are many ways for an employee to defraud the company. Four prominent ones are discussed below.

Direct purchases. Depending on their job level, employees may have the authority to make purchases on behalf of the company within certain dollar limitations. A dishonest employee might abuse this trust by purchasing items for one's personal use.

Vouchers. After an employee makes a business trip, it is necessary to submit a record of expenses in order to get reimbursed. You always have some latitude in recovering reasonable expenses that you incur on behalf of the company.

Generally, you aren't required to report your expenses in minute detail, and receipts aren't required for *all* expenditures (especially small ones). The case of the "Vanishing Hat" illustrates such latitude and how abuses might get started.

While on a company field trip to Chicago, an engineer's hat blew off his head and into a busy downtown street. Before he could recover his hat, it had been run over several times by the fast-moving traffic. It was completely ruined. Because it was cold in Chicago and he needed something to cover his head, he bought another hat of comparable value and saved the receipt. Upon returning to his base location he submitted a voucher that included the receipt for the hat he purchased. His boss refused to approve the voucher, his reason being that a hat was a personal item of clothing and hence not a reimbursable expense. The employee disagreed vehemently. He argued that if he hadn't been on the company field trip in the first place, he wouldn't have lost his hat. His boss countered by saying that it was the individual's responsibility to care for his personal belongings and it was not company policy to cover personal losses. All further arguing by the employee was to no avail, and he had no choice but to redo his voucher, omitting the expense for the hat. When the revised voucher was submitted, the boss noticed that the charge for the hat had, in fact, been deleted but somehow the total for the reimbursable expenses remained the same as the total on the original voucher. How could this be? He then read the note that the engineer had clipped to the voucher. It read, "All of the receipts that the company requires are attached to this voucher. All of my arithmetic is correct. The hat that I lost is somewhere imbedded in this voucher; see if you can find it." The boss gave in and signed the voucher.

Things turned out all right in this particular instance, but it may not always be the case. Several dangers exist. First, any unilateral action taken by an employee to compensate for differences between incurred expenses and reimbursed expenses is illegal, whatever the justification. The first transgression sets the stage for other abuses that completely lack justification. The second danger is that employees may be misled into thinking that if the boss signs off on the voucher, then it must be okay. On the contrary. You can get into the worst kind of trouble after the voucher has gone past your boss. Your boss is your friend. If he or she spots something amiss, most likely your boss will question you about it directly and resolve the issue without anyone else getting involved. However, once your boss signs off on the voucher, it becomes an official document and violations detected beyond that point may be interpreted as fraud. You can get both you and your boss into deep trouble. Finally, being able to produce receipts doesn't impress anyone. The receipt has to be for a business-related expense as defined by the company. You may be able to produce a receipt that looks like it is business related even though it isn't. Auditors are trained to spot the difference. It may surprise you, but I know of cases where company vice-presidents have been fired for falsely submitting receipts on items no more significant than auto-parking fees. The intent of the transgressor and the trust level violated are more important that the amount of the fraud.

Use of company material and property. It is a common practice to take home company pens, stationery, and notebooks. These small thefts dull our sense of honesty and pave the way for more serious infractions. Personal use of the copying machine, phone, company car, and company computer are progressively higher steps on the stairway to uncontrolled abuse. It is best never to take the very first step on this slippery pathway.

Theft of time. Theft of time takes many forms: Falsifying time cards, conducting personal business on company time, taking long lunch hours, putting in short work days, and phoning in fake illnesses are all ways of stealing time.

Theft of company time is perhaps the most prevalent form of white collar thievery. One trap you want to be sure to avoid is the "playtime" lunch hour. If a company is large enough, you will find within it groups of people who participate in fixed lunchtime activities every day. These activities range from playing cards to jogging, and they typically consume a major portion of the lunch hour. There are many reasons why people engage in them. Some typical reasons I've heard are, "It helps me break up (shorten) the work day," "It relaxes me," "I can't find any other time to do it," "I enjoy it," "It helps me clear my mind and think better," "I need something to look forward to during the day." Whatever the reason, it doesn't change the fact that such habitual activities can hurt you in two ways. First, they can tarnish your image. Employers like to feel that their workers' minds are totally on the job. It may rub some of them the wrong way to see groups of people playing games at work (even during scheduled breaks) while pressing business issues remain unsettled. This immediately raises doubts about your priorities and dedication to the job.

A second way the playtime lunch hour hurts you is that it can make you look like a time thief. Many people fall into the habit of devoting virtually all of their lunch period to their fixed activity and then scramble at the last minute to grab a bite to eat (sometimes going so far as to eat at their desks or in meetings). Others avoid this conflict by eating while participating in their fixed activity. In both cases, however, all of the lunch period is consumed every day, thereby leaving no margin for taking care of personal business on lunchtime errands. On days when personal business must be attended to, the lunchtime players often extend the lunch period into company time.

Although abuse of the lunch period is probably the most common form of time theft, most managers don't try to monitor such theft; they don't need to. They already have a good feel for what you should be able to accomplish during a typical week. Over a period of time, managers can gauge whether or not you are devoting full-time to the job by looking at your productivity. If it is down, then either you are inefficient or you are stealing time. Either one is bad and will lead to the same result.

Some companies encourage lunchtime activities and even go so far as to provide facilities to support them. That does not mean, however, that your *local management* looks favorably upon *your* participation in them. It may be difficult to find out exactly how your boss really stands on this issue, for if the official company policy permits it, but the boss is personally against it, he or she may respond to your inquiries by only stating the company policy and not revealing his or her personal bias. The only sure way to tell how your boss feels is to observe whether the boss engages in such activities.

In a nutshell, avoid falling into fixed nonbusiness lunchtime routines. Such activities can cause you to be stereotyped as a goof-off and tempt you to steal time from the company. Even though others may do it, it doesn't mean that it is right for you. Play it safe. Keep it strictly business during the day until you know for sure what is acceptable and what is not.

All of the above forms of theft are well known to the company. Most employees are not aware of the safeguards and invisible systems of checks that are in place to detect such abuses. It may look all so easy, but the company has had to deal with all forms of theft for a long time. You won't be able to invent any that the company has not seen or stopped. It is a risky business.

The company may let small thefts go unchallenged. Your immediate supervision may look the other way if they detect a small transgression. They might decide that it is not serious enough to fire you and they would just as soon avoid an unpleasant confrontation. The company security and assets-protection organizations are quite busy and must concentrate their efforts on the worst offenders. They may have documented proof of your guilt but may choose not to spend several weeks investigating a thirty-dollar crime. They may simply pass the information along to your management. Your management may do nothing. And because you hear nothing you may believe that your small theft went undetected. This can be the first crack in the disintegration of your career. You may be encouraged to repeat your offense and increase its magnitude. At the same time, you may be losing the trust and confidence of management.

FOLLOWING PRESCRIBED COMPANY REGULATIONS

As described in Chapter 1, most large companies have written regulations outlining the procedures to be followed in conducting business. These procedures may apply to personal matters, purchasing, promotions, business trips, or any aspect of company life. Although it is understood that it is the employee's responsibility to have a general knowledge of these procedures (and to know where to look to find specific information), it is also the employee's responsibility not to deliberately circumvent these procedures for one's personal gain.

Professional Reputation

Your reputation is based on past performance. As a new employee you haven't had the time to establish a long-standing record of excellence on the job. Your initial reputation, therefore, must be based on your performance in college or on prior jobs. Gradually, however, your performance on your current job will displace other inputs.

TECHNICAL COMPETENCE

Technical competence is the ability to do state-of-the-art work in your area of specialization. Basically, this is your ability to apply your academic training to real-world problems.

CREDIBILITY (VERACITY AND THOROUGHNESS)

As indicated in Chapter 1 in the section on oral communications, credibility is destroyed by bluffing. This is because bluffing is usually transparent. You can avoid the temptation to bluff by thorough preparation. Do your homework by anticipating what questions might come up and seek out the answers in advance. Identify the fundamental assumptions that your work is based on and check out their validity for the case at hand. But beware. Even when you do your homework, sometimes questions will come up that you can't answer. In these situations, remember that the work situation is different from school. You don't have to have the right answer right away or flunk. Remember that the standard response is to admit ignorance and follow this quickly by offering to seek out the requested information as soon as possible.

Remember, too, that reputation is momentum. It sustains you through valleys of subpar performance, but in time can be used up. It is a continual responsibility to keep your momentum going.

Communication Skills

People tend to confuse intelligence with the ability to speak fluently. In fact, the dictionary definition of someone who lacks the faculty of speech is "dumb." The meaning is different but the association remains. The association of intelligence with verbal fluency and articulation is so ingrained that it is virtually impossible to convince people that you are intelligent unless you can speak well. Furthermore, even if you have the best solution to a problem, it is hard to convince others that you are right unless you can effectively articulate your ideas. Thus, the ability to communicate, both verbally and in writing, is a high-ranking determinant in technical performance.

WRITTEN COMMUNICATIONS

As discussed in Chapter 4, the two most prevalent types of documents are memos and letters of correspondence. Doing a good job on these is virtually all that is necessary to convince others of your writing ability.

ORAL COMMUNICATIONS

You are always on review for your oral effectiveness. During day-to-day discussions, meetings, and technical presentations you are being evaluated on how lucidly you can express yourself and how cogent you can make your arguments. You thus should be continually practicing oral skills—even when it doesn't seem to count.

Productivity

Productivity is the product of work volume times the quality. Both elements are important. In gauging productivity the key questions that must be answered are: "What percent of my time was spent on work that was ultimately useful?" and "What was its value to the company?" Another thing that must be kept in mind is that productivity is not something that can be stored in the bank. You must continually ask yourself, as your employer might do, "What have I done lately?"

Leadership

Stripping away all the glitter and mystique, leadership means gaining results through others. Your leadership ability is important to management because it makes it that much easier for management to achieve the results that they desire through you. The more influential you are, the more effective they become.

Dedication

Dedication means having a personal commitment to the company. This commitment is reflected in how you treat your job: Punctuality, dependability, and being a hard worker are all signs of dedication.

Attitude

You hear all the time about how important a good attitude is, but hardly anyone bothers to define it. In fact, a good attitude means different things to different people and varies from one situation to another. A person's disposition and set of responses in one situation may constitute a good attitude, whereas the same behavior in another situation may reflect a bad attitude. In the workplace, having a good attitude means primarily: (1) expressing a positive outlook toward your job and the company, (2) demonstrating genuine interest in the well-being of the company, and (3) being responsive to requests and receptive to suggestions from supervisors.

One manifestation of a good attitude is that you don't let petty issues get in the way of getting the job done; that is, you don't bring excess baggage and hidden agendas to the job that make you hard to deal with.

Putting it succinctly, a good attitude means exhibiting a "can do" spirit toward your job and a spirit of cooperation with management and co-workers.

CALIBRATION OF PERFORMANCE LEVELS: HOW TO MAKE A SELF-ASSESSMENT ON HOW WELL YOU ARE DOING

The items listed in the previous section represent the range of parameters that most employees are graded on. This section attempts to lay out the associated grading scales for those parameters that lend themselves to quantification. Items such as ethics and attitude are difficult to quantify (that is, they are pass/fail items), have already been discussed at length, and are not treated again in this section.

Quantification of Technical Competence

The basic question to be answered is, "What is the quality of your work?" There are three ways of measuring this: Impact on company profitability, performance level with respect to your peers, and degree of significant documentation that results from your work.

Some managers take a very pragmatic view and contend that the only relevance that technical competence has is how it affects the company's profit or loss. Using this line of reasoning, an indication of competence might be obtained by quantifying how an individual's contributions have helped the company's market share or profitability. The trouble with this approach is that there is not always a one-to-one correspondence between your work quality and how it affects profitability. For example, a person may make a minor improvement in a product's design or manufacturing process that results in a small cost savings per unit. But because of large production volumes, the net savings may be large. Such a contribution may not be ranked as highly as excellent work on a more difficult problem that does not result immediately in returns to the company. Nevertheless, the idea of using increase in profitability as a surrogate measure of technical capability has some merit. This concept is most useful in continuous-process-type work where payoffs tend to be more immediate and the impact of innovations can be more precisely quantified.

A more widely used way of evaluating work quality is to make peer comparisons. In this case some of the questions that management asks about your work are:

- Was this a job that anyone could have done?
- Did the job require any extraordinary insight or ability?
- What was special about his/her contribution on this project?

- Was the project completed successfully? (that is, Were objectives met? Were schedules met? Did it sell?).

Another means of measuring work quality is the relative significance of the documentation that results from the work. There are roughly five levels of significance. Listing them with the most significant first, they are:

1. Publication in a professional journal.
2. Publication in a trade journal or in the notes of a trade conference.
3. Publication in the company newsletter or magazine.
4. Documentation in an internal memo.
5. No documentation at all.

In most companies, 4 is par. Extending the golf analogy a bit further, this makes 3 a birdie and 1 a double eagle.

Still another means that some managers use to rank competence is to compare it to an objective standard of performance (that nevertheless must be subjectively assessed). The performance scale is as follows:

RANKING	PERFORMANCE CHARACTERISTICS
Outstanding	Identified and solved problems and kept management informed.
Good	Identified problems and proposed good solutions.
Satisfactory	Identified problems.
Poor	Could not identify problems.

Continual maintenance and development of your skills are necessary to ensure technical competence. This means that school is never over. New employees especially should look for opportunities to take in-house courses that relate to their particular job specialty. Two to four such courses during the first two years on the job are not unreasonable.

One final word on quality and competence: Most companies grade on the curve. Your performance level is viewed with respect to what others are doing around you. Absolute performance levels often vary between different organizations in the same company. The best indicator of how management will view the quality of your work is to compare it with the quality of your closest peers.

Gauging Your Communication Skills

You can tell how good a writing job you are doing by the color of your documents when you get them back with your boss's comments on them. If only spelling errors are corrected or some technical facts challenged, then you are doing great. If, on the other hand, many of your sentences are reworded, paragraphs restructured, and large sections deleted, then you are in trouble. If the document is returned without any changes but with a note that says something to the effect that it needs reorganization, then that means that your boss has given up on it and you are in desperate need of a writing course.

Managers are a much misunderstood lot. It is not really true that they dislike reading drafts of your letters and memoranda (actually, it is one of the fun parts of their job). Rather, it is that they don't like correcting them. Trying to polish a rough diamond is tedious and time-consuming work. Not only that, managers and supervisors have to try to do it without badly bruising the writer's ego. For these reasons they often procrastinate in getting back to you with their list of comments and changes. You should be warned, however, that when you do get the document back, no matter how perfect it was to begin with, it is sure to have at least one item that needs changing. A fundamental law of corporate proofreading is:

Any draft submitted to management will contain at least one error. If none exists, they will create one.

You may be curious as to the phenomenological basis for this law. The reason has nothing to do with managers' egos or the presumption that they are just downright hard to please. It is just that managers want to make sure that you appreciate the fact that they spent considerable time and effort reading every blasted word of your document. A direct way of demonstrating this to you is to find something that needs correcting—the deeper in the body of the paper the better. Of course, not all managers do this every time, but all managers have been guilty at least once, even if they didn't realize it.

How are you expected to put up with such outrages? A former boss of mine, Bob Weiner, shared with me a tactic he developed to combat needless changes.

One of Bob's previous managers was notorious for sending back every document with at least one change. If his boss couldn't find a legitimate error, he would suggest some change as a matter of style. Now Bob was an excellent writer and felt rather bruised after going through this routine a number of times. He decided that something had to be done. After discussing the problem with some of his colleagues, he came up with an effective countermeasure: He deliberately planted an error for his boss to find. Bob explained that finding the obvious error should satisfy his boss's need to make a correction and thus prevent him from doing serious damage to the memo. After proofreading and correcting all errors in the draft of his next document, Bob went back and inserted an obvious typographical mistake in the middle of the document. He then submitted the draft to his boss. It worked. The boss found the planted error and left the rest of the document alone. Bob achieved his objective, and he continued to use this technique on every draft. The planted errors were always something rather benign, like a typo or a misnumbered reference, that would not reflect badly on Bob. It always worked.

The moral is that the amount of rework that you have to do on your documents after getting them back from your manager is a rough, but not foolproof, indicator of your writing effectiveness. By all means, take your writing seriously and try to avoid structural mistakes, but realize that much is a matter of style and don't get too bent out of shape by minor changes.

It is a bit more difficult to get a reading on what others think of your oral skills. People tend to be less brutal in critiquing speaking skills than written ones. Somehow the way one talks is a bit more personal than the way one writes, and hence, criticizing someone's speaking ability comes closer to making a personal attack on the individual. People therefore tend to be more polite and gentler with their criticisms.

The best indicator of how well you are doing during a presentation is to read the crowd reaction. The degree of attentiveness tells you if you have matched the content and level of the talk to the audience. Their reaction to subtle humor on your part is indicative of how well you have established rapport. If people are making frequent glances at their watches, then you know you are losing their interest and you need to end as quickly as possible.

The audience reaction after a talk also says something. A long silence after you ask for questions could mean a number of things—most of them bad. For example, it could mean:

1. You've confused them so much that they can't phrase an intelligent question.

2. Your ending was abrupt and caught them off guard.

3. You have overstayed your welcome and no one is about to ask a question and give you a chance to go rambling on.

4. People have given up on getting an honest answer from you.

5. They sense that you are uncomfortable and they don't want to prolong your ordeal.

6. They are asleep.

You can guard against this closing embarrassment by using some of the ending techniques described in Chapter 4 that alert the audience that you are approaching the end of your presentation.

Sometimes when you finish the audience hasn't had enough time to collect its thoughts well enough to ask insightful questions. In those cases you can stall for time for questions to crystallize by posing questions of your own. Since you have already thought about possible questions the audience might ask, you can say: "One of the questions I thought you might ask is. . . ." Then proceed to answer the question. If that doesn't stimulate the audience you should employ your favorite departing phrase and exit as gracefully as possible.

Good speakers are in high demand. If your talk results in spinoff requests to give similar talks, then you can conclude that you have done a good job. Such requests can come from your boss or from someone in the audience.

In other cases the only honest feedback you may get is during a performance review. Here you must be alert to what is really being said as opposed to what you want to hear.

Measures of Productivity

As already stated, productivity is the product of work volume times the quality. As we have just discussed quality, the remaining element is volume.

There is a tendency in industry to associate productivity with volume of documentation. Although this is clearly, by itself, an invalid indicator, documentation is important. It helps the company by providing a record of the work so that other employees can make use of it. It benefits the individual through personal recognition. The key factor concerning documentation is that it should be appropriate. By appropriate, I mean that it should be *timely* and *well done*. The page count is unimportant. It is worth repeating: Timeliness and quality of documentation are better indicators of productivity than volume.

As a final word on productivity and documentation, it is important to stress that writing is one of those things that can be done during slack times. The often dreaded job of documenting at the end of an assignment can be made less burdensome if you keep up as you go.

Signs of Leadership Ability

One measure of leadership is how effective people are in getting things accomplished through others who don't report to them. This is a rather objective test of leadership. When others follow your lead without managerial coercion it speaks highly of your ability to identify a winning course of action and to get others to buy into your ideas.

People are deceiving themselves if they complain that they could get more done if they only had more authority. Just being the boss doesn't mean that people will do what you want.

After all, a boss can't *make* an employee do anything. Employees are very creative when they wish to avoid a disagreeable task: They can engage in malicious obedience; that is, comply to the letter of your order, whether it makes sense or not. They can uncover more urgent crises to attend to. They can come up with reasons to be away from work (business trips, illnesses, vacations). They can find reasons why the objectionable task is not a good thing for the company to do. And finally, they can just plain procrastinate. Sure, if everything else fails, the boss can fire the employee, but the boss still would not have gotten the employee to do what was asked. And besides, employees who comply under duress are not likely to attack work enthusiastically, and the quality of the work will suffer. Thus, leadership has nothing to do with having people report to you. You can show leadership at any level.

You can assess how much leadership you are exhibiting by answering such questions as: "How much of my work gets done through the cooperation of others?" and "How much am I influencing the work of others?" In his study entitled "The Manager's Job: Folklore and Fact," Henry Mintzberg (1975) reported that managers, even up to the top executive level, only spend about 48 percent of their time managing subordinates. Thus, it seems that operating at, say, half this level would demonstrate management potential.

Assessing Your Dedication

There are two indicators that reflect dedication: (1) initiative and (2) how well a person works with little or no supervision. Dedicated people view job problems as their problems. Accepting this ownership, they take the initiative to address problems as they arise. This is in contrast to just recognizing a problem, reporting it, and waiting for someone else to do something about it. You can get a reading on your initiative by asking yourself how many loose ends are lying around on your projects for which no action plans have been put into motion. That portion of your work that accounts for 80 percent of your responsibility should have no unaddressed loose ends. Self-motivated people don't need the external stimulation of watchful management in order to work well. They tend to do more than what is asked, work long hours, and anticipate what needs to be done. You can gauge your effectiveness in this area by asking yourself these four questions: (1) What additional effort have I put on my projects that were not explicitly requested by management? (2) Do I put in whatever hours the job requires or do I spend the last half hour of each day watching the clock and leave on time, come what may? (This is one of the traps of a carpool) (3) How frequently have I correctly anticipated a question that my boss might ask and dug out the answer before meeting with the boss? (4) Do I work just as hard when the boss is not around? You need to have positive responses to at least three of these questions to consider yourself self-motivated.

HOW YOUR NONTECHNICAL CONTRIBUTIONS FIT IN

Nontechnical contributions include recruiting, public relations work, teaching a company course, participating in company clubs, and working on special committees. Although such work can enhance your technical contributions, it must be quickly pointed out that efforts in these areas cannot substitute for your primary responsibilities. Put another way, they can make a good technical effort look better, but they cannot make up for (or provide an excuse for) a poor one.

Work in extracurricular areas can benefit both the employee and the company. First of all, it *is* a service to the company. Though it may fall into the category of "something that anyone could have done," nevertheless, *you* were the one who did it and the company gained through this service.

The individual can benefit in several ways. For a new employee this offers opportunities to demonstrate leadership ability. Although the issues being dealt with vary from one arena to the next, the common element of leadership is dealing effectively with people. In nonjob-related areas there tends to be greater opportunities to assume immediate responsibility on projects requiring a great deal of interaction with people. Thus, the opportunity to show leadership is greater. Another factor is that, because such jobs enlarge your range of interactions, they automatically increase your visibility. Finally, performing in a number of different arena rounds out your image and shows versatility.

SUCCESS FORMULA IN INDUSTRY: SUMMING UP

Having gone through the material in this book up to this point, it should be obvious to the reader that there is not a simple set of rules that a person can follow to assure success in industry. Success is based on your making a full range of contributions and being able to work effectively in a variety of situation. There are, however, a few central issues. These issues are reiterated here to reinforce their importance.

Get an Early Start

There is a great deal of truth in the adage, "First impressions are lasting impressions." It therefore is important to make that first impression a good one. Review the chapters on "Things to Learn," "Skills to Acquire," and "Things to Do." Quickly get up to speed in these areas and maintain your momentum throughout the first year.

Be as Complete a Ball Player as You Can

Every employer expects new employees to have the ability to do the special job that they were hired to do. But this is only one dimension of performance. Excellence in other areas can multiply your worth. The first part of this chapter ranked the value of various facets of your total contribution. Communication skills are among the most important. Show that you can talk and write and that you willingly do both. Dedication is the next most important item, but this base is automatically covered if you get off to a fast start. Leadership ability is the remaining high-payoff attribute. If you can, try to hit all bases.

Stay in Tune with Management

Give management the benefit of the doubt. Assume that your boss knows what he or she is talking about and listen to that person. But do more than that: *Hear them.* Hear the message that your supervisor is trying to deliver and don't be preoccupied with your own agenda. This is not to say that you can't volunteer relevant information and raise important issues as appropriate. But don't let such exchanges keep your boss's message from getting through to you.

Alert supervision to potential problems in time for them to do something about them. Don't keep the bad news to yourself. The bad news won't get better. Delays in dealing with setbacks will only make it more difficult to recover gracefully. Remember, anyone can make a mistake, and new employees are expected to make more than others.

Keep your boss informed. Don't let him or her be blindsided with bad news.

Remember the golden rule of management: "He (or she) who has the gold, makes the rules." Translated, this means that you will have to satisfy your boss on the boss's terms and not yours alone. In negotiations with your boss, your chances of success are greatest when you can deal from a point of common interest. Try to stay in step with your boss and pull with, not against, him or her.

Get Some Responsibility for Some Portion of an Important Project

It does you little good to give a world-class performance on a dying project. Not only will it not be fully appreciated but some people may actually take the negative view that your efforts represent an unwise expenditure of company resources. Your talents need an adequate showcase. If you don't already have it, fight for some portion of the hottest project around. It doesn't have to be a major part to begin with. It is even all right if you have to work on it on your own time. The important thing is to get it. Your boss will understand when you tell him or her that you want to be in touch with those projects that are important to the company's future.

If you aren't successful in getting a foothold on one of the hot projects, then you should consider transferring to a different organization or changing companies. It is better to do this early rather than late. Kept in the shadows, your skills erode and your market value declines.

WORDS
OF COMFORT
TO PEOPLE NEW
TO THE
BUSINESS WORLD

Don't be intimidated. Although life in industry is different from life on campus, it is seldom overdemanding. No one expects you to be a genius. Your college training has prepared you well enough to succeed if you are willing to work. Most of the people that you will come in contact with will be human beings, just like your college peers, and perhaps more seasoned. They won't eat you alive. Despite the differences, you will be able to relate to them on most issues. If you keep your nose clean and establish good communications with your boss and co-workers, you can handle the professional challenges as they come.

The workplace is an arena where you will be presented with many new challenges, choices, and opportunities to perform. You have the potential for incredible contributions, and you will discover that your individual efforts do, in fact, make a difference. You will also find that working with others is a means for amplifying both the quality and magnitude of your contributions. You will experience the rewards that come from group success that are seldom felt with individual achievements. Although it is real and for keeps, it is also a fresh start and a chance to write your own success story. Good luck.

BIBLIOGRAPHY

ARONSON, ELLIOT, AND JUDSON MILLS, "The Effect of Severity of Initiation on Liking for a Group." *Journal of Abnormal and Social Psychology*, 59 (1959): 177-81.

BRUSAW, CHARLES T., GERALD J. ALRED, AND WALTER E. OLIU, *Handbook of Technical Writing* (2nd ed.). New York: St. Martin's Press, 1982.

DOMHOFF, G. WILLIAM, *Who Rules America?* Englewood Cliffs, N.J.:Prentice-Hall, 1967.

FLESCH, R., *Art of Readable Writing* (rev. ed.). New York: Harper & Row, 1984.

GUTEK, BARBARA A., *Sex and the Workplace.* San Francisco: Jossey-Bass, 1985.

MILLS, C. WRIGHT, "The American Business Elite: A Collective Portrait," in C. W. Mills, *Power, Politics and People.* New York: Oxford University Press, 1963, pp. 110-39.

MINTZBERG, HENRY, "The Manager's Job: Folklore and Fact." *Harvard Business Review*, 53 (July-August 1975): 49-61.

PASCALE, RICHARD, "The Paradox of 'Corporate Culture': Reconciling Ourselves to Socialization." *California Management Review*, 2 (1985): 26-41.

PFEFFER, JEFFREY, "The Ambiguity of Leadership," in *Psychological Foundations of Organizational Behavior*, 2nd ed., (Barry M. Staw, ed.). Glenview, Ill.: Scott, Foresman & Company, 1983, pp. 282-89.

REIS, H. T., L. WHEELER, N. SPIEGEL, M. N. KERNIS, J. NEZLEK, AND M. PERRI, "Physical Attractiveness in Social Interaction: II. Why Does Appearance Affect Social Experience?" *Journal of Personality and Social Psychology*, 43 (1982): 976-96.

ROSEN, ELIZABETH A., *Putting It All Together: Working Toward Career Satisfaction* (Unpublished notes on career pathing in the corporate environment, AT&T Bell Laboratories, 1985, Short Hills, N.J.).

STRUNK, WILLIAM, AND E. B. WHITE, *The Elements of Style*. New York: Macmillan Publishing Co., 1979.

U. S. BUREAU OF LABOR STATISTICS, *January 1983 Current Population Survey*. Washington, D.C.: U. S. Bureau of Labor Statistics Office, 1983.

WARNER, W. L., AND J. C. ABBEGLIN, *Big Business Leaders in America*. New York: Harper and Brothers, 1955.

WATERMAN, R.H., T. J. PETERS, AND J. R. PHILLIPS, "Structure Is Not Organization," *Business Horizons*, No. 80302 (June 1980).

INDEX

A

Abbeglin, J. C., 38
Acknowledging the work of
   others, 107–8
Advancement, opportunity for,
   19–20, 91–93
  going back to school and.
   39–41
Advice/help from:
  boss, 30, 31, 37, 44, 46
  co-workers, 117–18
Affirmative action programs, 7
Ambience, company, 19
Appraisal. *See* Performance
   evaluation/reward system
Aronson, Elliot, 18
Assignment(s), individual job:

company mission and, 9–11
following up on, 130–31
getting assigned to an important project, 95–96, 153–54
your first, 24
AT&T, 4, 6, 91
Attitude, positive, 93
  performance evaluation/
   reward system and, 143

B

Baden, John, 117
Bell, Alexander Graham, 4
Bell Laboratories, 4, 91
Boss, your:

of you, from boss, 126, 127
Culture, corporate, 21, 93
Customer satisfaction, achiev-
ing, 102

D

Dedication:
performance evaluation/
reward system and, 143,
152
self-assessment of, 150–51
Defrauding/stealing from the
company, 136–40
Delivery dates, meeting, 100
Desk organization:
avoiding desk congestion,
61–62
bulletin boards, 61
calendars, 60–61
files, 59–60
notebooks, 62
Domhoff, G. William, 38
Dress, 103–4
Drugs, 103

E

Economy, sense of, 84–86
Education:
company programs, 7, 95
going back to school, 39–41,
95
Equal Employment Opportunity
Commission (EEOC), sex-
ual harassment and, 42
Ethics:
defrauding/stealing from the
company, 136–40
following prescribed company
regulations, 140
performance/reward system
and, 136–40

Evaluation, personal. *See* Performance evaluation/
reward system
Evaluation of the company:
absolute versus relative,
17–18
advancement, opportunity for
personal, 19–20
ambience, 19
culture, corporate, 21
geographical match-up, 20
health and stability, 19
how to tell if it is the right
place for you, 17–22
job match-up, 20–21
leave or stay, how to decide
to, 21–22
mainstream of the company,
how to get plugged into the,
22–24
management, astuteness of,
18–19
personality compatibility, 21
quality ranking, 18–20
Expectancy Theory of motivation, 32–35

F

Face-to-face, speaking, 111
Files, 59–60
Following up on assignments,
130–31
Ford, Henry, 4
Ford Motor Company, 4
Foresight, 83–84
Friends, co-workers as, 119–20

G

Geographical match-up, 20
Grading. *See* Performance
evaluation/reward system

P

Pascale, Richard, 3–4, 18
Peer(s). *See* Co-worker(s)
Performance evaluation/reward
    system:
    advancement, opportunity
        for, 19–20, 39–41, 91–93
    attitude and, 143
    boss and, 24, 25–28, 126–29
    co-workers, avoiding com-
        parison with, 26
    dedication and, 143, 152
    ethics and, 136–40
    how it works, 11–13
    how to deal with, 25–29
    informal feedback, 24, 36,
        127
    leadership and, 142–43, 152
    nontechnical contributions
        and, 151–52
    oral communications and,
        141–42, 152
    perks, 12
    positive aspects of, 29
    principal determinants of,
        135–43
    productivity and, 142
    professional reputation and,
        141
    providing your own input,
        127–29
    raises, 12
    salary, 12, 91
    self-assessment, 143–51
    subpar performance and, 91
    unfairness and, 25–28
    written communications
        and, 142, 152
Perks, 12
Perri, M., 44
Personality compatibility, 21
Personnel department, 8
Perspective, sense of, 84
Pfeffer, Jeffrey, 38

Phillips, Julian, 3–4
Phone calls. *See* Telephone
    routines
Planning, avoiding faulty, 78–79
Productivity, 98–99
    performance evalua-
        tion/reward system and,
        142
    self-assessment of, 149
Propriety, sense of, 84

R

Raises, 12
Reis, H. T., 44
Reputation, your professional,
    141
Resourcefulness, 80–82
Rewards. *See* Performance
    evaluation/reward system
Risk management, 85–86
Rosen, Elizabeth, 6, 91
Routines and regulations:
    corporate, 5–6, 140
    personal, 55–62, 110–11

S

Salary, 12, 91
School, going back to, 95
    deciding on, 39–40
    impact of, on your job, 41
    opportunity for advancement
        and, 39–41
    part-time versus full-time,
        40–41
Self-assessment, 143–44
    of dedication, 150–51
    of leadership, 149–50
    of oral communications, 147–
        49
    of productivity, 149